D1612399

BELFAST

Paintings and Stories from the City

Paintings by Gillian Boyd
Text by Fred Heatley

Cottage

Publications

First published by Cottage Publications,
Donaghadee, N. Ireland 1998.
Copyrights Reserved.
© Illustrations by Gillian Boyd 1998.
© Text by Fred Heatley 1998.
All rights reserved.
No part of this book may be reproduced or
stored on any media without the express
written permission of the publishers.
Design & origination in Northern Ireland.
Printed & bound in Singapore.

ISBN 1 900935 09 0

THE AUTHOR

Born and raised in Belfast's 'Sailor Town', Fred left school at 14 years of age to work as a message boy. From here he moved into engineering through which he progressed via sowing-machine mechanic to ship repairs. from factory installation and maintenance to engineer in the printing trade.

A keen sportsman in his youth, he played soccer and boxed in both the amateur and professional rings. Later a keen youth hosteller where he cycled and fell walked.

During the 1960s he began contributing articles on sport, current affairs and local history to various newspapers and magazines. Down the years his work in the field of local history has gained recognition, (this will be his eighth publication) and today he is regularly called upon to give talks on and lead tours in both his native city and elsewhere in Ireland. He has also contributed to television and radio, and for several years served as a governor of the Linenhall Library.

THE ARTIST

A native of Newtownards, Gillian has spent most of her college and working life in Belfast.

She attended Regent House School from where she graduated to Duncan of Jordanstone College of Art in Dundee before returning home to complete her degree in 'Combined Studies in Art and Design' at the University of Ulster, Belfast.

Gillian's preferred medium is watercolour and/or ink and, although for the illustrations in this book she has kept to a representational format, she can work equally effectively in a traditional or contemporary style. Indeed in her spare time she has built up an excellent portfolio of vivid sketches and paintings for children.

Gillian has exhibited at numerous group and solo exhibitions, though due to demand, much of her work is painted to commission.

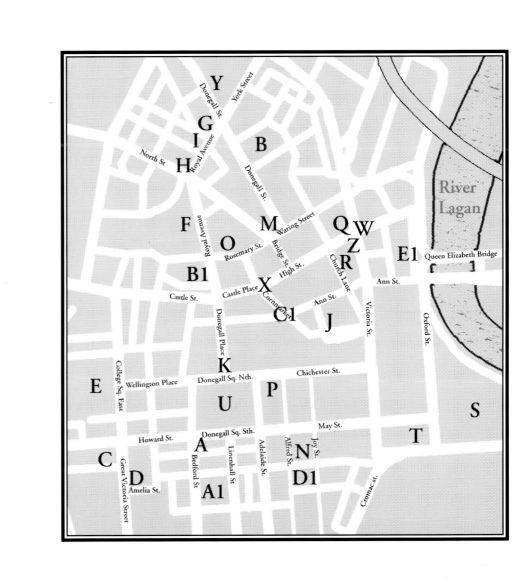

CONTENTS

The Origins of Belfast   **3**

Paintings and Stories from the City

THE ORIGINS OF BELFAST

The site of Belfast has been described as being in the shape of a shovel, with one high and one low side. To the east there are the low hills of Castlereagh feeding back towards Drumbo, and on the opposite flank the high escarpment of Cave Hill and on to Divis and Black Mountain. In between, there is the base of the 'shovel,' widening out to meet the waters of Belfast Lough, and it is on this level floor the city was to develop. Not, as is commonly believed, on the banks of the River Lagan but on the banks of a tributary of the Lagan, the Fearsat (Fearsad, Farsat or Farseat) which rises on the high ground north-west of the city and, after flowing south-east turns directly east dividing our Falls and Shankill before emptying into the Lagan where it once met Belfast Lough near the bottom of our present High Street. It is from this location on the Fearsat that the city takes its name, from the Irish *Beal Feirste* meaning the 'mouth, or entrance, to the sand-banked river', literally to a sandbank on which the river could be forded.

That ford was actually across the then much wider and shallower Lagan, somewhere in the vicinity of St. George's Church. Through time *Beal Feirste* corrupted to Belfast, but it is completely erroneous to include a bell in the arms of the city, as that instrument had nothing whatever to do with the origin of the settlement.

Geographically, the formation of the city's site goes back some 5,000 years when the land which forms this lower end of the Lagan Valley finally settled down. There had been a turbulent few millennia prior to then, beginning with the end of the last ice-age about 12 000 BC. The millions of tonnes of water cascading off the higher ground was blocked as it gravitated down into what we now know as Belfast Lough as the lough itself was still frozen from about Holywood to Whitehouse. The melt-waters were then compelled to back up and created what in geological terms became 'Lake Belfast,' a huge expanse of water covering inland as far as today's Kings Hall at Balmoral and Ballymurphy on the foothills of Divis.

During pre-glacial times the River Lagan had flowed to the west of its present course, taking in what is now Dunmurry and entering what is now Belfast on a route close to Falls Road. But the mammoth pressure of ice from Scotland still pressed on the north of Ireland, leading to an eventual breach by the dammed waters of 'Lake Belfast' eastwards through the Dundonald Gap and on to Strangford Lough. This rush of water led to the forming of the Malone Ridge, an immense barricade of fine sands washed down to the bed of 'Lake Belfast.' The River Lagan, finding its old course impeded, took a line of least resistance by twisting round behind the ridge at Malone to find its current route. The former course of the Lagan is still traceable, almost 60 metres (approximately 200 feet) under the Bog Meadows which remain between the Falls Road and the Motorway. These meadows are kept moist by several small streams which flow into and through them, the most notable being the River Blackstaff.

The Scottish ice pressure finally eased about 5,500 years ago and the northern section of Ireland, roughly from County Meath to County Sligo, lifted and created the landscape which exists today. In the to-be Belfast the inland waters receded, leaving districts once flooded to a depth of some 3 to 7 metres (10 to 20 feet) high and reasonably dry. But the lower ground remained damp, and for several millennia what is now central Belfast must have been passable only in seasons of dry weather, and even then with difficulty. The warmer climate had its own problems with its encouragement to tree and shrub growth in the hollows and on the flanks of the hills. In such conditions the movement of people or animals was really only via the rivers or on natural eskers, or sand ridges.

The earliest evidence for human habitation in Ireland goes back only to 7 000 BC compared to some 250,000 years in southern England. In the north of this island the earliest site so far uncovered is that at Mount Sandel at the mouth of the River Bann, near Coleraine. First noted in the 1880s, it not was not until the 1970s that a full excavation was carried out enabling a fuller dating and pushing evidence of people in Ireland a thousand years further back than previously thought. At what stage those Mesolithic people reached the Belfast area may never be satisfactorily answered with current belief being sometime in the fifth millennium BC. A site uncovered on the Lagan near Ormeau Bridge in

1892, and written up by the Rev. W. A. Adams in the *'Ulster Journal of Archaeology'* of October 1898, was the first indication of so early a date: that Ormeau Bridge finding was corroborated by the discovery of a similar-age site in Sydenham.

Both of those locations were at almost shore level, but the majority of later (Neolithic and Bronze Ages) finds were located around 150 metres (500 feet) up the western mountain side of Belfast, and a at similar height, or almost on top of, the opposing range at Castlereagh. Hill forts predominated with the Giant's Ring above Edenderry village on the Lagan, outstanding. At a period when marsh matted the low ground and forest and scrub the higher, this Neolithic site (defensive or ceremonial ?) was surely significant in its closeness to the waterway of the Lagan and its magnificent view of the land around.

Of immediate importance to the early settlers was movement from one sector to another. Never easy in the natural environs of the time, it was necessary to take advantage of whatever was provided in the way of eskers, or on the higher ridges above tidal mark. And with the knowledge of how the landscape was long ago it has been suggested that several of Belfast's current main thoroughfares follow tracks laid down in the distant past by those settlers. The east-west axis takes in the Newtownards Road and on to North Street and over Peter's Hill to the Shankill ; the north-south axis is less evident, though it can be accepted that passage northwards was on the high ridge from Millfield, across Carrick Hill to North Queen Street and on over the heights at the Grove and Skegoniel. At low tides advantage was surely taken of the shore itself.

Rivers and streams posed problems and none more so than the major one, the Lagan. It was not on the Lagan that Belfast was to rise but on the Fearsat, the southern bank to be precise. A natural land spit exists framed by three rivers - Fearsat, Lagan and Blackstaff and its extent can be easily gauged: the Fearsat flows culverted beneath High Street; the Lagan until well into last century covered what is now Victoria Street and the land reaching down to Donegall Quay, and wall plaques at Dublin Road and at Ormeau Road, on the Gasworks site, indicate where the Blackstaff runs. Much of this area within the river boundaries was liable to flooding but it was the nucleus of Belfast, particularly the dry ground fronting the Fearsat.

Origins

There is no absolute surety as to when Christianity reached Belfast, but what is accepted is that the earliest church was at Shankill (the name is from the Irish, meaning *old church*) located within the grounds of Shankill Graveyard. First mentioned in 1306, there were attached to this mother church six chapelries, one of which was the 'Chapel of the Ford' believed situated on the present St. George's Church site and thus adjacent to the ancient fording place. Tradition tells that this little church was to facilitate those desirous of crossing at this most northerly place on the Lagan separating the future counties of Antrim and Down: a prayer for a safe crossing was made by those wading the nearby ford and from those who had successfully made the journey in the opposite direction, a prayer in thanksgiving. Being subject to the tides of the lough, the ford was always potentially dangerous, never more so than when the Lagan was in spate. It was this fording which gave birth to Belfast, its importance being recognised as later centuries brought struggles for land and political supremacy.

But long prior to then, in the throes of pre- and post-glacial times, Nature had laid down the materials from which the incoming city was to benefit. Covered by the basalts which cap the Antrim Plateau there is a deep bed of chalk stretching from Divis to Squire's Hill, at Ligoniel, which due to its flint containments was of immense importance to the earliest inhabitants, the flint providing arrow heads, scrapers, knives and other necessities of the age. And when, from the 17th century onwards, the shortage of good building stone led to a reliance on brick from which to construct housing and factories and whatever, suitable material was there in the 'sleech' or Estuarine Clays which predominate the region. Those bricks gave Belfast a distinctiveness commented upon by so many visitors.

Deep natural wells provided good drinking water, and the mineral waters for long identified with Belfast. And, if reliance can be placed upon the interpretation of the old place names, there was once an abundance of oak available which must certainly have been an incentive for the early ship builders: names such as Edenderry, a large townland taking in the modern Ardoyne to Clonard, tells of the 'ridge of the oaks' and Derriaghy, in the south-west, speaks of the 'field of the oaks.' The volume of water flowing in such as the Fearsat and in the Connswater at Ballymacarrett gave power to the water-wheel driven and, later, steam-driven mills which put the city to the fore in cotton and linen production. A sheltered port, linked by gaps in the surrounding hill and mountain ranges to interior markets, gave the Belfast site advantages over most other settlement areas in Ireland, advantages which, in industrial terms, were to be accepted with great acumen.

D ue, perhaps, to the influence of Albert, Prince Consort and husband of Queen Victoria, who we are informed had an interest in such things, the Scottish Baronial style of architecture proved popular in Belfast. This may have been the reason some of the business elite in the city chose this style when they consulted architects about a new building. Or it may simply have been, as in this building, a Scottish company reflecting their heritage. Whatever, this former Scottish Temperance Building was erected to the plans of Henry Seaver and completed in 1904, thus adding to a series of new buildings girding Donegall Square. A *"free treatment of the Scottish Baronial style"* is how one commentator (C. E. B. Brett) has it, whilst another (Paul Larmour) described it as *"more French chateau than Scottish castle"*. But it remains a symbol of Belfast at its commercial zenith, when the city could brag of having within its precincts some of the largest industries in the world.

As business premises replaced housing around the White Linen Hall and its replacement City Hall, so their owners gave overt expression of their wealth, with, unlike modern times when structures with squares of glass and steel line our roads, hard cash was allocated for decoration, even if the result was more troublesome than the worth. Bedford Street, Linenhall Street and the smaller streets linking them formed what was known as 'Linenapolis' where the linen manufactured in factories elsewhere was hemmed, sewn and embroidered into garments or table and bedlinen for the home and overseas markets. The extremely hard and tiresome work in the mills was principally carried out by women who, up to the mid-1950s could be seen any morning or evening heading to or coming from their places of employment. But the introduction of the man-made fibre industry made linen a luxury, and all luxuries have a limited outlet. 'Linenapolis' died, almost overnight. Many of the older buildings were pulled away and replaced by higher and less ornate structures, some of which are less than pleasant to the eye. Utilitarian but, with rare exceptions, hardly an adornment to any city.

A lot of the workers in 'Linenapolis' came from the nearby Markets or Sandy Row districts, and the self-containment of the area was evident. Each street had its complement of hem-stitching rooms; there were sewing-machine dealers in both Linenhall and Bedford Streets; there was a maker of wooden crates in Linenhall Street and also a large stationers wherein could be obtained cardboard cartons. There was even a post office in Donegall Square South to enable dispatch to customers. A business oasis within a business city.

DONEGALL SQUARE SOUTH

The first building known to have occupied this site was the original Brown Linen Hall, not too long after the street was new to the town of Belfast and from which it was consequently named Linen Hall Street. But the Marquis of Donegall, though an absentee landlord, insisted the new church which he wanted to replace the dilapidated St. George's in High Street, had to be on this site, then on the northern limits of the town. So, down came the Brown Linen Hall to find a new situation further along the street on the opposite side, and work commenced on the church which was to bear the name St. Anne, Anne also happening to be the name of the first wife of the Marquis.

It was a handsome enough building with a nice tower, a tall spire and a fine Classical pediment. But someone had boobed; an outside clock positioned on the tower in a recess behind the pediment was difficult to see unless one was quite a distance away. So, down came the clock to be repositioned some feet higher up, on the tower directly in front of a window light. Illustrations show a circular recess appearing incongruously behind and just above the pediment, whilst up above a timepiece which seems to have been pinned awkwardly like a badge upon a coat lapel. Anyhow, that early St. Anne's, commenced in 1774, was completed two years later and served its Church of Ireland adherents for well over a hundred years.

As Belfast grew in importance it was felt that a Cathedral should be incorporated within its bounds and the St. Anne's site looked most suitable. The problem was, what to do with its regular worshippers? A few hundred yards further up Donegall Street the Catholic St. Patrick's clergy had a similar problem when they set out to replace their small, original church; a problem solved when they took away the accoutrements on the exterior and erected the nave of the new church around the shell of the old, enabling services to be held until shortly before full completion. This procedure was followed at St. Anne's with the last service in the first edifice being held on the last day of 1903, and on 2nd June 1904 the nave of the new Cathedral was consecrated. But it was to be almost 80 years before the work was completed with, in the meantime, eight different architects being engaged.

A second sharing with St. Patrick's is that each place of worship has a body interred within its walls: first was St. Patrick's with the burial of Bishop Patrick Dorrian (d.1885) and in St. Anne's that of Sir Edward Carson (d.1935).

The Cathedral will forever be associated with its 'Black Santa' and his assistants who, whatever the weather, collect for charity on its steps at Christmas.

ST. ANNE'S CATHEDRAL

When Ireland's second rail line, that between Belfast and Lisburn, was commenced in 1839 it was incumbent that both ends should have a proportionally ornate terminus; Belfast went overboard. In 1848 it was formally opened - probably to the design of the Great Northern Railway Company's engineer, John Godwin - a huge and memorably draughty station which ended its days as the northern link with Dublin. By the 1960s, decisions were being made to run down the rail network throughout Northern Ireland, yet it was with surprise that the G.N.R. was levelled and a site selected for a new Central Station which was anywhere but central for the majority of its users. And to compound that lapse of judgement, in recent years a junction has been made to the main line, once again bringing it to Great Victoria Street.

But one's loss can be another's gain and the eleven-storied Europa Hotel sprouted where the G.N.R. station had been. The time chosen for its construction proved not the most fortunate as 'The Troubles' were commencing with horrific ferocity and the Europa felt the blasts more than most. On over 40 occasions it suffered from bomb or arson attack giving it a world-wide fame which its management could have done without. The new prestige building was almost inevitably a target, plus the belief that several reporters, allegedly reporting from frontline positions, were in fact safely ensconced within the security of the hotel. The Europa survived, though at one period there were genuine fears that it would close leaving central Belfast bereft of first-class visitor accommodation.

Another feared casualty of the bombing was the Grand Opera House, one of the city's prime attractions. A Frank Matcham construction, it has all the exuberance associated with his work. Its opening in 1895 was announced with great flourish by its manager, Mr. Warden, who,

> "begs to announce that the .. magnificent building will open to the public on Monday next, December 23rd. One of the most beautiful and substantial structures in the three kingdoms. Frank Matcham, architect, London; H. & J. Martin, contractors, Belfast. After the overture, the national anthem will be sung by the entire company. ... The theatre will then be declared open by Lord Arthur Hill, MP. and Mr. J.F. Warden will address the public: after which will be produced Messrs. Dottridge & Loudens'...BLUE BEARD; OR, IS MARRIAGE A FAILURE?..."

Successful for many years in live entertainment it opted to become a cinema, but the theatre's design mitigated against modern cinematic operation and it closed down in 1972 to lie vacant for several years. It was, however, a listed building and following extensive and expensive restoration it opened once more for live entertainment. The overhang at Great Victoria Street is an addition to Matcham's original work, part of the restoration by Robert McKinstry. The contractors were again H. & J. Martin.

GRAND OPERA HOUSE
& EUROPA HOTEL

It has been stated that John Betjeman, British Poet Laureate from 1972 until his demise twelve years later, was a passionate admirer of Belfast's Victoriana, and it has also been stated, that he enjoyed a tipple. If both statements are true, then the Crown Bar must surely have been early on his itinerary whenever he visited the city. The Crown bears further distinction in that it is the only working public house in Ireland, perhaps anywhere, owned by The National Trust who have Bass Ireland maintaining it for them.

Established in 1839-40 as the Ulster Railway Hotel it was obviously timed to coincide with the opening in 1839 of Ireland's second railway line, linking Belfast with Lisburn. Terence O'Hanlon was proprietor during the 1870s, but most identified with the early Crown was Michael Flannigan who, in 1885, had the interior gutted and the marvellous one there now, installed. A couple of years later he had the tiled façade added, both works by the local architects E. & J. Byrne. Whilst in more modern times pub owners have generally removed all vestiges of age, including the once-obligatory snugs, the Crown owners have shown much more foresight. Their belief that keeping up with modernity can include a blending of styles, with as much of the old as possible retained, has resulted in an interior, and exterior, as nearly late-Victorian as can be envisaged. The pub has long been so famed that, as far back as 1946, Carol Reed thought it worthy of inclusion in his film *Odd Man* Out, based on a story by Belfast-resident novelist F. L. Green. But, contrary to general belief, there was no actual filming in the Crown - a mock-up in an English studio was utilised. The numerous bomb attacks in Great Victoria Street caused damage to the exterior, but fortunately a pattern for the original tiles was found and Robert McKinstry was able to effect an accurate restoration.

As to be expected with the railway opening up links throughout Ulster and points south, there was a need for daily and overnight accommodation in the vicinity. Two doors from the old Ulster Railway Hotel was the Dublin and Armagh Hotel. Opened in 1846, it was to become Robinson's, another favourite Belfast bar. Tragically, it suffered severe fire damage in the spring of 1991 and what we have today is a reconstruction. The Crown and Robinson's are complementary, as is The Beaten Docket, just across Amelia Street from The Crown. That, too, had originally beenan hotel, The Downshire Arms, owned by W. J. Finnegan, and opened in the late 1850s. Amelia Street itself had its quota of small two storeyed boarding-houses, buried in the shadows of the nearby linen warehouses. It is maybe better recalled as a hangout of *'les mademoiselles de la nuit'*.

CROWN BAR & ROBINSON'S BAR

Though facing on to one of the busiest traffic junctions in Belfast, the Royal Belfast Academical Institution ('Inst' to those on more familiar terms) retains a distinct aura of quiet and solemnity. It may be that the hedged lawn in front and the sheltering to north and south by, respectively, the early-century College of Technology and the modern Jury's Hotel confer a privacy which its location would otherwise prevent. Built with the aim of educating ministers for the Presbyterian Church, it has always adopted a much wider outlook and provided a haven of tolerance in what was often a less-than-tolerant city. The date in Roman numerals above the main entrance is for 1810 and it was in July of that year the foundation stone was laid. But it was March 1814 before pupils were admitted to the new college with grounds and building being *"dreary-looking ... grassy lands on all sides, and numerous dead walls in blocks of streets which had received names and were partially occupied"* as one entrant, George Benn, historian of Belfast recalled it. The grand plan had been of a new college in the midst of a grand square; the intended south and west sides of which failed to materialise. The sides that did materialise were occupied by academics and the people of wealth with some of their dwellings, many radically altered, still standing. The opening of 'Inst' must have had a bearing on the siting of the town's first museum overlooking it and that museum, (no longer providing its original function) now operates as a cosy little theatre and a gallery for various exhibitions.

However the tolerance of those associated with 'Inst' did not forever meet with the approval of all, and one individual in particular who resented it was Dr. Henry Cooke (1788-1868), a noted Evangelical Presbyterian who was greatly opposed to the Unitarian precepts of the Institution. In that period of religious argument, Cooke's voice was powerful and his supporters numerous. So much so that when he died the statue of the young Earl of Belfast, which had stood on the plinth directly in front of 'Inst', was removed and one of Cooke erected in its stead and it is said that Cooke stands with his back to 'Inst' as a deliberate snub to those who refused to accept his arguments.

Perhaps the most amazing point is that Cooke's statue is known far and wide as 'the Black Man' which title belonged, instead, to that of the young Earl. When he died and a statue, by Patrick McDowell, was placed in situ in 1855, it was, for some unexplained reason, painted black. Cooke's supporters had it removed and it stands, almost unnoticed on the first floor of the City Hall at the head of the twin stairs. Down the years, Cooke's bronze statue (by S. F. Lynn, 1875) has adopted a natural green patina yet such is the obduracy or colour blindness of Belfast folk that it remains 'the Black Man.'

R.B.A.I &
'THE BLACK MAN'

Royal Avenue takes in what were originally Hercules Place, Hercules Street and John Street. By the mid 19th century its rabbit-warren of alleys and laneways and its numerous butchers' shops had become the Catholic sector of Belfast being close, as it was, to St. Mary's Church in Chapel Lane and not too far from St. Patrick's in Donegall Street. It was a less than salubrious area and the over-crowding caused by rural people fleeing the Famine and seeking work in industrialised Belfast led to unhealthy environs. It was then possibly a desire to kill the fabled two birds with the one stone which led Belfast council agreeing to pull away the old thoroughfares and open a grand vista to Cave Hill, matching the pride of a town heading towards cityship.

Those with good memories will recall some of the more splendid buildings which lined the route: the opulent Grand Central Hotel, the fine General Post Office, the Royal Avenue Picture House and the many smaller shops and premises between. At the rear there was the romantic Smithfield Market and a huddle of little shops and houses which somehow retained the sentimentality of their construction. But the bombings of the 1970s destroyed some of those and a decision was taken to remove postal affairs to a new building in Gamble Street and a new central post office in Castle Place. The Army was billeted in the old hotel and access to Royal Avenue was restricted by manned barricades at all approach routes with the consequence that trade and life was stifled.

As the troubles eased and normal life resumed, there was concern in expected circles at the announcement that a huge shopping complex was to embrace all of the premises listed above. But its construction, at a cost of £63 million by Building Design Partnership for John Laing plc, went ahead. It took five years to build and in 1990 opened as Belfast's largest shopping mall. As with most such undertakings it needed an internationally recognised 'anchor tenant' and Castle Court was successful in this respect by attracting Debenham's.

Of typical glass and stainless steel construction it occupies a vast amount of ground, quite a section being absorbed by a multi-storey car park at the rear. Yet inside the mall it is surprisingly intimate. For shoppers there is a wide variety of wares on offer, though most are unaware that above the two-floored shopping precinct there is a third floor which provides office accommodation for various bodies.

CASTLE COURT

The 'Belfast Evening Telegraph' (the 'Evening' dropped from the title in 1918) was the first halfpenny newspaper in Ireland and, the sixth evening newspaper in the British Isles. Its publishers, brothers William and George Baird, were from Randalstown and in 1861, purchased the stock and goodwill of the Ulster Printing Company in Belfast's Arthur Street. From there, on September 1st 1870, they published their paper which was of decidedly Conservative views. As the political turmoil of the late-19th century deepened and Home Rule for Ireland was the dominating issue, so the 'Belfast Evening Telegraph' strengthened its Unionist beliefs to become the voice of Unionism and its associated Orangeism.

Its power increased as the Bairds expanded their business by establishing such as the 'Ballymena Weekly Telegraph' and the 'Larne Times' they also published a sporting paper, 'Ulster Saturday Night', which in 1895, thirteen months after its initial appearance, became 'Ireland's Saturday Night', having Belfast and Dublin editions. With several daily editions of their main sheet, a 'Weekly Telegraph' and their rural satellites, the Bairds were to prove one of Ireland's most progressive newspaper entrepreneurs. When the old John Street was converted to become a section of the new Royal Avenue, they acquired a large site to which they moved in 1886 to a building specially designed for them by Henry Seaver. As the years went by that building was extended to enable installation of more modern machinery.

Being Northern Ireland's only evening newspaper they hold a monopoly which has never been challenged but, somehow, they never attempted to operate in the morning or Sunday markets until October 1988 when the 'Sunday Life' rolled off their presses (although some years earlier they had tried, without success, to buy the then-ailing 'Newsletter'). By that period the structure of the Telegraph had altered. The Baird family control had been lost when, following the tragic death in a motor-racing accident of Bobbie Baird, grandson of founder William Baird, in 1953, and a long and often acrimonious legal battle, the titles passed to the ownership of Thomson Regional Newspapers in l960/61, this being the first of the Belfast newspapers to go out of local hands.

But more obvious to the readers was the stance initiated in the 1960's by the then editor, Jack Sayers. Though himself a staunch Unionist he set out to soften the long-held hard-line Orange/Protestant/Unionist attitude of the Telegraph and attempt to mend fences in an unfortunately divided community. Obviously there was dissent among readers and some staff at this deviation, but Sayers' policy has been maintained to the present day.

BELFAST TELEGRAPH

From Gin Palace to reputable banking establishment is quite a leap, but such has been the experience at the north-western corner of North Street and Royal Avenue. As early as the 1870s a James Connolly had a Gin Palace here. He, however, died young (thirty-nine years old) in May 1885 and his Gin Palace passed to the ownership of J. J. McDonnell who held possession from 1899 until 1924. A large, three storeyed building, it was then purchased by the Bank of Ireland who engaged McDonnell & Dixon of Dublin to provide them with an additional premises in Belfast. The Bank, founded by Act of Parliament to stabilise the somewhat unstable Irish economy, opened its first branch, in Dublin, in 1783, coming to Belfast in July 1825 when an agency was set up. As Belfast continued its inexorable growth to become Ireland's manufacturing capital, so the Bank of Ireland and other banking companies hastened to expand their presence there. Proper bank buildings were built but, uniquely, it is only in fairly recent times that the Bank of Ireland agreed to refer to those in control of their branches as 'Managers' rather than the former less-prestigious 'Agents'.

The Gin Palace was pulled away and under the direction of Joseph V. Downes, architect, a new Art Deco structure rose in its place. Completed in 1930, its geometrical and rectilinear lines and the use of Portland stone make it one of the more pleasing architectural features in the city. Its corner site took advantage of what were once among Belfast's most commercialised thoroughfares with both streets lined with shops and offices and with small manufacturing firms nearby. The city's principal library and all of the local newspaper offices were also close by, each adding an attraction to financial entrepreneurs.

Long prior to then, this was the northern limit to the town and the old North Gate in the ramparts which enclosed the hamlet, was situated hereabouts. The eventual removal of those ramparts and the expansion of Belfast to and beyond their limits meant the expansion of Hercules Street into John Street and onwards via York Street to Carrickfergus and points north. John Street, not to be confused with the more modern street of the name (off Divis Street), joined Hercules Street in being demolished to form Royal Avenue and is all but forgotten today. A narrowish way stretching from North to Donegall Streets, it was renowned as somewhere where board and lodgings could be found. In 1820 three such facilities are listed and fifty years later, shortly before it ceased to exist, there were ten, and for those who needed cash in a hurry and had something worth pledging, there was also a pawnbroker.

BANK OF IRELAND
ROYAL AVENUE

Libraries have long been a feature of counties Antrim and Down, in earlier times usually referred to as 'Reading Societies' or 'Book Clubs', and they were located in districts which even today are of relatively small population - Doagh, Ballyclare, Carnmoney, to list some - with members willing to make payment to read, or listen to others read the latest newspapers, pamphlets or the heavier publications. In Belfast, the Society for Promoting Knowledge (the Linen Hall Library) was founded in 1788 and seven years afterwards came one of the more enterprising rural groups, the Banbridge Reading Society, which was to exist for almost fifty years. At a period when large accumulations of books were principally the preserve of the literate wealthy or in church or college libraries, the collection of the Banbridge Society was quite extensive comprising, in 1838, no less than 1,586 books plus a large selection of pamphlets, an indication of support for the written word in that particular locality.

But libraries are not necessarily only for those who can afford the fees asked and in 1850, The Public Libraries and Museums Act came into force, applying to Ireland three years later. But it was almost another three full decades before the Act was adopted in Belfast and the following year, 1883, W. H. Lynn won a competition held to build the town's first public library. The site chosen was in the old John Street and resulted in the removal of premises belonging to a publican, a baker, a butcher, a brazier and gasfitter, a provision merchant and a grocer. Local builders, H. & J. Martin, were contracted for the work, but a series of disputes and the loss of material on its way across the Irish Sea, prolonged the construction leaving it to 1888 before the library's doors opened to the general populace. That year, coincidentally, was when Belfast graduated from town to city and the emergence of the new library added to the celebrations. In its formative years the library doubled as the city's museum with, in the 1970s, a huge addition being made to the rear to house its newspaper holdings. Those holdings had had a somewhat nomadic career being formerly in Shankill Library and prior to that at Donegall Road. Within the new central extension they could be properly spaced, micro-film machines installed and decent facilities for users provided.

Libraries in Belfast have been provided by some surprising outlets such as two of the city's principal shopping stores, Anderson & McAuley and Robinson & Cleaver. In parallel, several church and political groupings also supplied reading material to their members. Of the latter, the Sexton Debating Society charged an admission fee of (in old money) six pence and two pence per month thereafter.

CENTRAL LIBRARY

The 1877 Belfast street directory lists a woman with a wonderful name, Harriet Eaglesfield, as publican at Nos. 39 & 41 Police Square known formerly as Poultry Square, now Victoria Square. Involved with those name changes were alterations in door numbers and it appears that Nos. 39/41 became today's No. 18 and the site of the Kitchen Bar. Established in 1859 it is almost ten years later before the earliest directory-listed occupant spirit dealer is shown, one S. Bell. Then we find Harriet Eaglesfield, followed by a Mrs Bell who was suceeded by the first of the Conlan family who held the premises for well over a century. Thomas Conlan was there by 1887, with Michael (c. 1911-29) and James (c. 1930) in train. By 1991, James T. Catney had taken over and his son, Pat, displayed an acute sense of local history when he held a series of talks, under the title of 'Old Belfast and A Pint' in the bar during April/May 1995. The talks proved popular, and few areas in Belfast are better placed for such a venture.

It is a quiet locale nowadays but once Victoria Square, and its predessesors were a hive of human activity. In 1823 there were 10 houses in Poultry Square containing a population of 33 males and 32 females. And Telfair's Entry (today's Telfair Street), which opens on to the square had 94 inhabitants in its 18 houses. A fowl market had given the place its name, that market taking place along the quays of the old May's Dock which fed in to the River Lagan. The dock was filled in about 1848 and by then Belfast's new Town Hall took up the square's corner with Montgomery Street. Opened in 1842 that civic amenity lasted only until 1871 when Anthony Jackson's newer (now Old) Town Hall in Victoria Street came into use. A former fish market outside the 1842 Town Hall had been converted to a morgue, with wits claiming 'no better place to cool tempers' in a heated council debate.

By 1880 Victoria Square had arrived and it was indeed a mixed bag of purposes. Conlan's bar was between Banquet Buildings, a fine, in style, whiskey store (pulled away in 1961 to build Churchill House) and a long established coffee stand belonging to the Irish Temperance League. Out in the middle of the roadway stood a large cast-iron, late Victorian public toilet for gents (removed in 1966), whilst at the bottom of the Square at Victoria Street was the Jaffe Memorial Fountain. Erected in 1874 by Sir Otto Jaffe in memory of his father, Daniel, it has in more recent times been sited near King's Bridge at Stranmillis where it goes almost unnoticed by those who pass it by. Across Telfair Street was the Empire Theatre of Varieties from where many of the entertainers made their way through Montgomery Street to Joy Street to find 'digs' for the night.

THE KITCHEN BAR

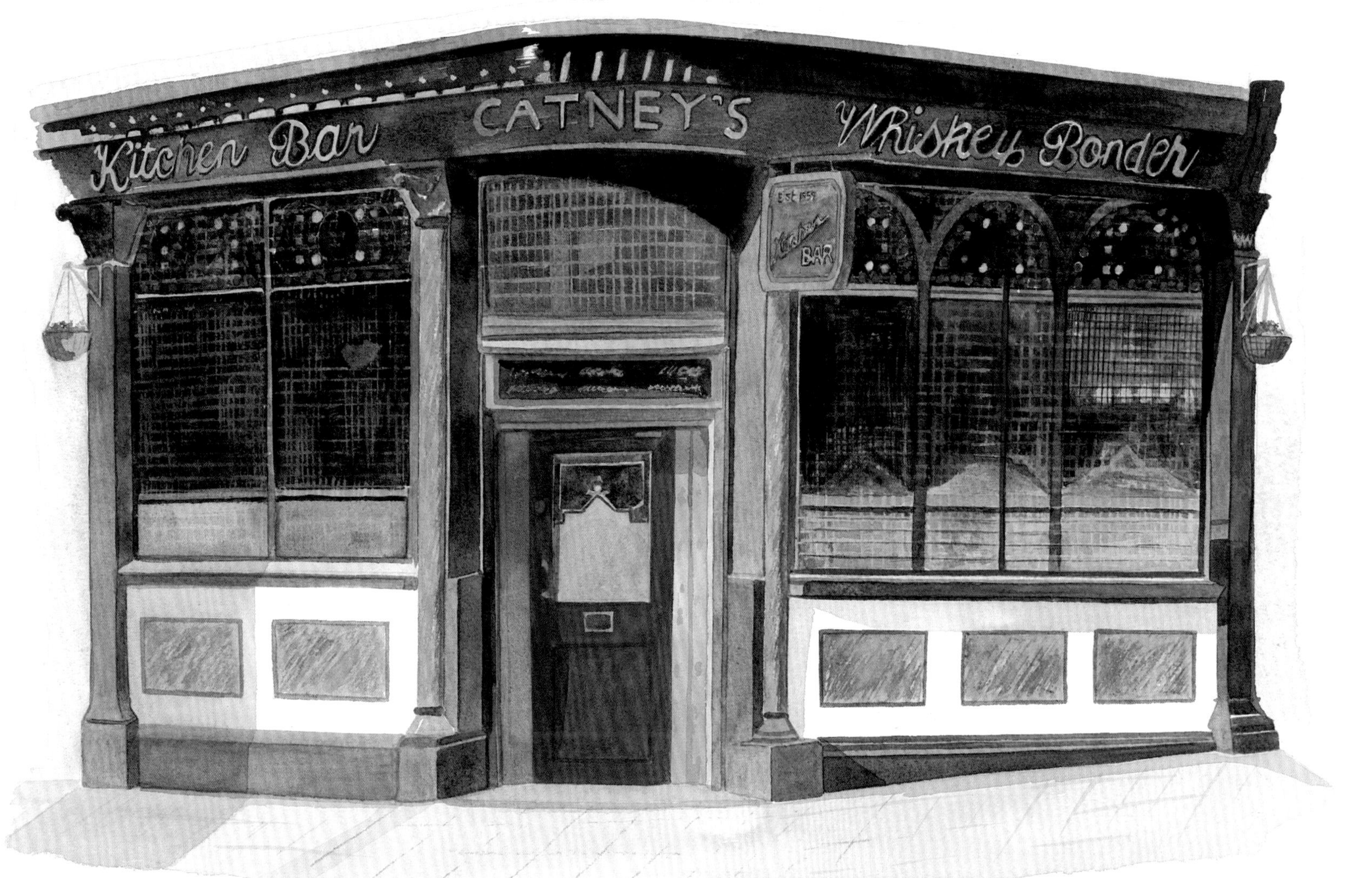
Kitchen Bar
CATNEY'S
Whiskey Bonder
Est 1959
BAR

Cast the mind back the best part of two centuries and envisage Donegall Place as the most desireable place in Belfast to have a home. The town was growing away from its older habitations on, or near, the Fearsat river which still ran without cover down the High Street, with many of the former dwellings upon its banks already turned to commercial use. A new cut had been opened, which because it led directly to the White Linen Hall had been named Linen Hall Street. Upon its route were erected large three-storied residences and it was here that 'The Quality' chose to live.

Among the early names were the physicians William Halliday and James McDonnell. The latter had strong associations with the 1792 'Harp Festival' in the Assembly Rooms. By 1820 there were the bankers John Sloan, Narcissus Batt and John Houston; the linen dealers Robert Nelson, John Sinclair and John S. Ferguson; the collector of excise and five times Sovereign of Belfast, Thomas Verner; at No. 1 Donegall Place was John Bunting, music master, and Mrs. Bunting who ran a boarding school. Fifty years later, commerce had moved in and the splendid old housing had been converted to shops or were in the process of being so. The last to be demolished was where Robinson & Cleaver were to erect their ornate emporium. A corner site with gardens and trees, it fell to the shopping trend about 1890 when Edward Robinson and John Cleaver engaged Young & Mackenzie to add another bay to their existing store.

The grandest house of all was that belonging to Lord Donegall who, to escape his creditors in England to whom he owed immense sums of money, had taken the ship for Belfast where he was to reside in a house, the side garden of which is now covered by Samuels the jewellers. It was quite a large residence, four storeys high, multiple extensions and innumerable rooms, plus the obligatory space for horses and coach. Donegall was, by all accounts, heavily in debt, yet he added to his property by acquiring a smallish country cottage at Ormeau which he extended to mansion-size and a hunting lodge near Doagh. It was that fecklessness with money that led to the breaking up of the Donegall patrimony and huge estate with his father-in-law, Edward May, obtaining a substantial slice of the land.

Of those fine homes of the late 18th century only the rudiments of one, now No. 25 Donegall Place, survives. This was one of three built by Roger Mulholland (1740 - 1818) for rental purposes, with Dr. James McDonnell being a tenant.

DONEGALL PLACE

The history of cities is often hidden away in entries and alleyways; the little throughways where the hand of the developer is less likely to strike. And so it is in Belfast. But we have lost quite a lot in recent years and whatever life remains in the city's entries emanates from the public houses which, in their own manner, provide hideaways and a little character for those who know where to find them. The 'Duke of York' in Commercial Court is one such. Paul Kelso, a dealer in wine, porter, ale and ginger and spruce beer, is listed as early as 1820, but whether this is the forerunner of 'The Duke' is difficult to prove. There has however been a tavern on the site since at least the mid-1860s. A 'rendezvous of the newspaper fraternity' it was here that the late, beloved Bud Bossence of the 'News Letter' held sway, and many of the would-be literary and political figures of his day gathered to listen to and to add their own conversation. That old hostelry suffered gravely from bomb damage in 1973 and had to be replaced, and was again upgraded as recently as 1992. The Court itself was once the abode of a select clientele with among its earliest inhabitants Hugh Brown, a violin maker and teacher of music and dancing, Josias Kerr, a teacher, and Mrs Keenan with her French and English school for young ladies. But by the end of the century it had become a dust-laden lane of commerce as no less than three flax and tow merchants had premises there. T. A. Scully owned what was the 'Duke of York', though the first mention of the title in the directories was when James W Gyles was proprietor just prior to The Great War.

Exchange Place, formerly Elliot's Court, has no reference to a tavern in its story, but away back in the 1820s it shared a population of 60 inhabitants - 25 male and 35 females in 31 dwellings - with its near neighbour, Commercial Court. Both lanes, narrow, square-setted with Mourne granite, capture a little of the flavour of an older Belfast. Indeed, this side of lower Donegall Street retains, badly mutilated as may be, some of the essence of the late-Victorian town. Exchange Place and Commercial Court obviously relate to the old Exchange and the commercial buildings further down the street.

Winecellar Entry originated from Bigart's Alley and dates back to the early 18th century. When the former Caddell's Entry and Legg's Lane were removed to make way for Lombard Street, Winecellar Entry became three-pronged with its side-opening into the new thoroughfare. The now-forgotten 'Belfast Mercury' was published at No. 6 in the Entry from its founding in 1851 until 1859 when it removed to Arthur Street, lasting only another two years. But it is 'White's Tavern' which bears most association with Winecellar Entry. Taking its name from Hugh White & Co. (established 1787) the modern title seems to stem only from the early 1960s, though this may well be the oldest bar site in Belfast having associations going back to 1630. Badly damaged by a bomb in the early 1980s it has been almost totally rebuilt.

BELFAST ENTRIES

Enclosed within the former Northern bank are the remains of one of the city's most historic buildings, the old Assembly Rooms. Opened in 1769 as a single storied market house with a fine arcade it was, under orders from Lord Donegall, raised in 1776 to include a room in which important events such as balls and meetings could be held. The site alone gave it importance as this was 'The Four Corners', a well known address in 18th century Belfast, the corners being those of Bridge Street, North Street, Waring Street and Rosemary Lane (now Street).

It was in the rooms that the lauded Belfast Harp Festival of July 1792 was held, a festival at which 11 harpers played their music to the gratification of those in attendance, except Theobald Wolfe Tone, then on one of his regular visits to Belfast. He was, of course, involved in more radical events, but to note in his diary of July 13 that it was *"... the Harpers again, strum, strum and be hanged ..."* hardly denotes musical appreciation.

There had been earlier gatherings of harpers at Granard in Co. Longford, but no attempt had been made to record the various airs. Belfast in its hard-headed way decided not to let the opportunity pass and engaged the young town-church organist, Edward Bunting, to note the airs. His notes are reputed to have inspired Thomas Moore to set words to the music and provide us with the once well-loved *"Moore's Melodies"*

Whatever the truth about Thomas Moore, there was not always harmony in the old Assembly Rooms as, during the frightful era of the '98 Rebellion, it was here that Henry Joy McCracken, leader of the Unitedmen at Antrim town, was tried. His family lived just a few minutes walk away in Rosemary Lane and great must have been their sorrow as the court sentenced their son and brother to death by hanging. His execution took place around the corner in High Street.

In 1845, Sir Charles Lanyon converted the premises to banking use for which purpose it has been used ever since. But a study of old illustrations showing the Assembly Rooms show that the conversion was sympathetically carried out and held reasonably well to the original façade. What had been arcaded entrances were partly built up to become windows and doors, but the interior was greatly changed to facilitate the new owner.

OLD ASSEMBLY ROOMS

It was an imaginative gesture by those responsible for naming the Fold in Hamilton Street after the nostalgic 'Chapel Fields.' Only the elderly will actually recall the 'Fields' being used, and then solely in the context of boxing during the 1930s. But they were in use from at least the turn of the century when at set times, such as Easter, they provided cheap amusement for the humble folk of the city. At that time there was still open space in front of St. Malachy's Church and though that space was not church property it was given the handy appellation of 'The Chapel Fields.' Facing almost directly on to the parochial house in Alfred Street they ran through to Adelaide Street with entrance from either thoroughfare.

In the early days it was bands, music, hoopla stalls and the fun of the fair. But in 1934 a new activity was introduced, one which was to dominate until the venue was closed down in late 1938 by order of the City Fathers. Boxing was the attraction and its promoter was not some bent-nosed veteran of the ring or some soft-hatted, fur-coated individual with a large cigar sticking from his mouth, but a woman – and what a woman! She was as tough as nails. Clare Copley, better known to all as 'Ma' Copley, was English and had settled in Belfast where she was to spend her remaining days. With a large leather bag strapped to her waist she collected the door money herself, and with entrance fees ranging from 3 old pence to 6 old pence (top price $2\frac{1}{2}$ pence in modern money) the fighters' remunerations were scanty enough. Yet when 'Ma' died in 1949 at the age of 84 there was a standing homage to her by the hardened Ulster Hall fans. At the 'Chapel Fields' she ran three shows every week and when moving to the Ulster Hall venue, introduced the regular Wednesday and Saturday fight nights.

The building of housing in the upper markets was much more sedate. Laid out in the 1830s in a grid-pattern, this was an area where the minor gentry could reside without the huge expense of gardeners, ostlers and other 'necessary' personnel. The houses were large enough to make life bearable, there was room for a servant or two and a stable entrance for the horse. Unfortunately, the 1970s witnessed the destruction of much of the district, though there was sense enough to restore some of the houses in Hamilton and Joy Streets. The latter has a special relevance as it was where, in the days when the Theatre Royal and the Belfast Empire Theatre of Varieties ('The Empire') were thriving, the visiting actors often found 'digs'.

CHAPEL FIELD FOLD

One of the stories associated with Rosemary Street (or Rosemary Lane as it was in older times) concerns the Rev. Sinclair Kelburn. Born in Dublin, son of Rev. Ebenezer Kelburn, he arrived in Belfast as assistant to the Rev. William Laird of the Third Presbyterian Congregation, and when Laird died he succeeded him to the post. Kelburn was a radical in political matters if not in theological (the two adjoining congregations were of the New Light persuasion whilst he remained Conformist) and on an occasion when the military in the town rampaged through the streets, Kelburn appeared in his pulpit the following sabbath in full Volunteer uniform, resting his musket against the pulpit door. For this defiance of political authority he was arrested and lodged in Dublin's Kilmainham Gaol from where he was released only after he had lost the power in his legs. Back in Belfast he retired from the ministry in November 1799 and died in 1802, his body being taken to the high hill at Castlereagh for burial in the churchyard there.

In 1832 Kelburn's old chuch, the Third Presbyterian, was replaced by a splendid new edifice with four magnificent cast-iron Doric columns and a range of wide steps leading up from street level. But in May 1941 that place of worship, with so many others throughout the city, was destroyed in the blitz which ravaged Belfast. Its congregation, however, was not completely dismayed and they almost immediately acquired joint possession with the Ekenhead congregation at their church in North Circular Road, and there they remain preserving the older name of Rosemary Presbyterian Church.

Rosemary Street has the privilege of being one of the oldest and most historical thoroughfares in Belfast. Among its most prominent past residents were the Drennans and McCrackens, members of both families having heavy involvement with the Volunteers and later United Irishmen. The Street was also unusual in that it once held no less than three Presbyterian churches in its short length, all within hearing distance of each other. There was the First Rosemary congregation established in 1642; then came Rosemary Second Presbyterian in 1707, followed by the Third in 1722. The latter two were lost in the 1941 blitz, with the Second Presbyterian site (immediately behind First) being turned into a car park and that of the Third being utilised to build a Masonic Hall (Young & Mackenzie, 1950s).

One of the towns earliest playhouses was in Rosemary Lane, and older folk may recollect the bombsite at the corner of Rosemary Street and North Street being occupied by a fun-fair in the 1950s - the *'Street of the Churches'* was not always religious.

ROSEMARY STREET
1ST PRESBYTERIAN CHURCH

It is difficult to imagine Belfast with a canal running through its centre, but that was once a serious consideration for the city. Linking with the already-existing Lagan Canal and making its way up what is now Chichester Street, past the White Linen Hall and through Wellington Place, it would have continued westwards via the fields now graced by the Royal Belfast Academical Institution. Luckily, the idea was shelved and the rural 'South Parade' was developed to become Chichester Street with four of the dwellings erected in 1804 still with us. These are remnants of Georgian Belfast of which little enough remains: the only comparable terrace we have is that in upper Donegall Street which was restored during the 1980s. Both short blocks are important as they are Belfast's only rivals to what has been preserved in Dublin, London, Bath and elsewhere. Four-storey over basement with Doric door columns and fanlights; it is a pity that No.11 has been altered at street-level to shop premises.

These are almost the last of the family homes which once clustered around, or were close to, the White Linen Hall. Around the corner in Donegall Square East are a couple of dwellings dating from c.1830, and in Donegall Square South there was (until bombed during the 1980s) the last of a nine-terrace block built by Adam McClean in 1808: McClean it was who owned much of the land hereabouts and who donated the ground for St. Malachy's Church. Nearby, in May Street, are some mid-century dwellings and these, added to those already mentioned, give some notion of how desirable this location was as a residential district. Close to business and yet having open countryside almost on the doorstep, as 'the Long Walk' leading over to the Blackstaff Rivers and Joy's Paper Mill ran up to the rear of the White Linen Hall.

The earliest known inhabitants of Chichester Street were, in 1807, Robert Baillie and Robert Caldwell, both described as 'merchants.' They, possibly, were in the housing replaced at the turn of this century by Ocean Buildings, thus leaving Chichester Street oddly beginning with house No. 5. By 1820, No. 11 was being shared by the Rev. William McEwen of First Rosemary Street Presbyterian Church and the linendraper, Alexander Nelson. By the 1870s the house had been divided into business premises though Nos. 5 & 7 were still in private occupation. Change was inevitable and as central Belfast became more commercialised families moved out to such as the Malone Ridge area. Interestingly, C. E. B. Brett who is so much responsible for awaking an interest in architectural heritage has his legal practice at No. 5 Chichester Street.

CHICHESTER STREET

There can be no dispute as regards Belfast's preeminence in the industrial record of Ireland. Cotton, linen, shipbuilding, engineering, mineral-water processing, tobacco manufacturing and rope-making made it one of the most significant centres in the history of the industrial world. It was all part of a grittiness and determination by industrialists to manufacture the best and to push their sales world-wide but, along the way, there were the inevitable inequalities leaving a residual distrust between employer and employee. This distrust led to embryonic trade unions emerging, based principally around the craft guilds, and to the formation in 1881 of the Belfast United Trades' Council. Since then the unions have had their part to play as work practices altered and the base of reasonably full employment in the mills, factories, shipyards, transport, etc. shattered.

In 1959 when Transport House was completed (architect J. J. Brennan) for The Amalgamated Transport & General Workers' Union there was still much employment available for non-skilled workers, the backbone of the TGWU. The site selected for their headquarters, whether by accident or design, could hardly have been more appropriate as it was close to the old Merchants Quay at which ships loaded and unloaded their cargoes right into the last century. As Belfast grew and wharfing facilities were extended, the number of workers soared and disputes became more regular, culminating in 1907 which began with the carters and ended with the local policemen also striking!

As union strength broadened so did the desire to have a headquarters which represented that broadening and this resulted in the acquisition of the present TGWU site. The five-storey building has, on the High Street frontage, a stylised representation of (from the top downward) an aeroplane, cranes, a ship, a bus and a line of workers as homage to those whom the union stands for.

Almost facing, across Victoria Street, is the former Northern Bank premises built by Charles Lanyon in 1852. Not his finest work according to C. E. B. Brett who notes that "*the general handling of the Italian style is rather clumsy*". This was the Bank's head office and its low-slung construction was at variance with its surroundings where the attitude was to build high on what, not so long before, had been tidal marsh. Though the Northern Bank vacated these premises in the early 1970s the TSB moved in and the long tradition of monetary care carried on.

TRANSPORT HOUSE

In these times of multi-national stores and shopping malls the days of the small shop grow ever shorter. Yet they do exist, and there is no better example in the heart of Belfast than Miss Moran's of Church Lane. A tobacconist has been in these premises for well over a hundred years with, prior to then, both Nos. 4 & 6 being shoe shops. About 1877, William McLarnon took over No. 6, moving from former premises in Washington Street. After a couple more years he gained No. 4, holding both until 1933. Residing at Fountainville Avenue, he was titled 'tobacco manufacturer', an elaborate enough title but one which can still be applied to the shop's present owners.

Tradition tells that the Misses Moran - there were apparently three of them - came to Belfast from Galway, although the date of their arrival is not quite clear. But in 1928 they are shown as living at Irwin Crescent, off the Newtownards Road. By 1930 at least one of them had acquired the tobacconists once belonging to Edward Kelly at 10 Church Lane which he had passed on to a Mr Kirk around the turn of this century. But Miss (or was it the Misses?) Moran moved along the terrace in 1934 to Nos. 4 & 6 and the name over the door has been there ever since. In April 1987 the Moran connection was ended when the present owners, the Elliott family, took over. They, wisely, have retained the old well-known name and on their shelves can be found for sale three tobacco mixtures which hail from earlier times. There is *'Dr. Johnson's Special', 'Miss Moran's Special'* and the oddly-titled *'W. 4'* which, on enquiry, turns out to be in reference to the street number of the shop! With its mahogany counters, its old tobacco advertisements and its tongue-and-groove walls and ceiling there is still an element of the older Belfast here.

This is one of the oldest throughways in the city. Dating from the 17th century, bordering the old town graveyard which surrounded the parish church, it was known as Schoolhouse Lane as the town's earliest recorded school, provided by Lord Donegall, was built there in 1665. Not a great deal is known about this school other than it seems to have been located at the corner with Ann Street. When, in 1902, work was being carried out on this site, the Belfast antiquarian Francis Joseph Bigger, requested of the workers that watch be kept for a grave close to the door of the old school, which he believed was where the local United Irishman, Henry Joy McCracken, had been buried. Bones were recovered and the discovery revealed to Robert May who had them carefully removed and brought to Bigger's home on the Antrim Road where they remained until buried in the McCracken grave in Clifton Street Cemetery seven years later.

MORAN'S TOBACCONIST

As with most urban centres, Belfast did not grow in a steady progression to a well thought out planners' decision: building here and there was sporadic as required. The spanning of the ground with housing between the little church at the junction of the Fearsat and Lagan and the castle, a couple of hundred yards away, would have been the first such undertaking. The industrialisation of the late 18th and early 19th centuries brought into existence many of the present-day inner and outer suburbs such as Millfield, Ligoniel, Andersonstown, Ardoyne and the greater Ballymacarrett. The introduction of the railways and the later tramway system extended the growth with much of that extension being 'ribbonised' in that it was a string of single houses connecting farmland to mill village and into the town itself. An expanding population meant not only housing, but schools, places of worship and entertainment. Thus what had been little gardens in the heart of Belfast were turned to commercial use or to more houses. In time, the large estates on the suburbs also fell to the developer.

These phases of development, industrial and residential, came and went as causes dictated. The commercial boom of the latter half of last century went flat after the 'Great War' of 1914-18. The shipyards almost died (one went out of existence) during the inter-war years and money became tight as the entrepreneurs held back and little of substance changed within the city. The blitz of 1941 which destroyed so much of the housing stock, the money generated by the war which provided a post-war surplus, and the need for replacement homes led to a renewal, at last, of the sub-standard housing throughout Belfast. The linen trade was all but gone and this added to the difficulties of the troubles of the '70s, '80s and early '90s meant a reluctance to invest in the city centre or, indeed, anywhere where there was a risk of bombing or arson. However, through government and other grants and an acceptance that the worst was over, building began again, often on a grand scale.

One of the sites selected for renewal was that lying on the city side of the Lagan. This had long been something of a waste land. The Lagan Canal, stretching from Lough Neagh, ended here at what was known to older folk as 'The Send Quay'. But the canal never proved financially viable, and for some unexplained reason developers had hesitated to erect houses overlooking the Lagan leaving it at its lowest reaches almost a cesspit. But the new weir – the first real attempt to control the waters of Belfast Lough and Lagan River as they merged – and the construction of the Waterfront Hall and the nearby hotels give life to what were livestock and fish markets – a sign of hope and confidence in the future.

WATERFRONT HALL

With its location at the foot of the Albert Bridge, close to the Queen's Bridge, almost on the River Lagan and being near to the centre of Belfast, this was an excellent site for a market. Over the bridges came the farming community of Co. Down with their cattle, horses, vegetables, eggs and fowl; from the Lagan and from the docks came the fishermen with their catches. From the town and surrounding areas came the buyers and many a hand-slap and many the luck-penny sealed bargains as cattle and horse dealers sold animals whilst the women 'flogged off' eggs in the traditional manner of adding to the housekeeping. But those days are long gone and St. George's Market nowadays is more regarded for its dealing in clothes and the usual bits and pieces which are on sale in such venues.

The original market which gave name to the vicinity was opposite St. George's, across Oxford Street on land now part of the Laganside development. This was May's Market, taking its name from a once well-connected Belfast family. The 1820 directory lists its proprietors as being the 'heirs of the late Sir Edward May' and it is through the Mays that we have today's May Street, May's Meadows and Maysfield Leisure Centre or, at least, the names. Not that the family bore any great honour as one writer has noted Sir Edward as being *"regarded as anything but respectable"* and another that *"for even in a corrupt age the conduct of Edward May out-herods Herod".* The latter was in relation to May and his friend, John Congreve, pocketing £15,000 between them for selling off their seats when parliament in London offered MPs cash to give up their seats so as to push forward the 1801 Act of Union.

In 1795, May had married off his illegitimate daughter, Anna May, to George Augustus Chichester, the future Lord Donegall, an achievement brought about by advancing cash to the forthcoming Lord at a most advantageous time. The May/Donegall connection paid as the former was able to acquire Belfast land at cheap prices including, presumably, the site for the market. Socially he hid his unsavoury reputation by being Sovereign of Belfast on six occasions and Member of Parliament for 14 years.

St. George's came later in the first half of the 1890s, at the behest of Belfast Corporation. J. C. Bretland was the architect, as he was for the former Fish Market beside May's Market and the Morgue on Laganbank Road. Though St. George's was utilitarian in concept, it bore its share of the adornments which made Victorian architecture so pleasant to gaze upon. Some of that adornment has weathered but with the market undergoing restoration we may witness its reconstruction.

ST. GEORGE'S MARKET

For many years the City Hall was a bone of contention among aesthetics due to its lack of formal architectural rigidity: in more modern times it isregarded as one of the more attractive buildings in Belfast. Its site, either from along Donegall Place from where it closes off the city's main shopping location, or from Linenhall Street which displays what some regard as the City Hall's finest view, was well chosen. But that particular site had been chosen for a smaller and less grandiose building, away back in 1784 when the current merchants of the town decided that the sale of the white, or bleached, linen deserved a hall worthy of the enterprise and of those involved in its promotion. Thus, on what was then the southern limit of Belfast was erected the White Linen Hall, the memory of which is retained in the Linen Hall Library which for several years had rooms in the building.

But as industries other than linen boomed throughout the 19th century and Belfast was granted status as a city in 1888 it was decided that the White Linen Hall had to go and a new, much more imposing edifice denoting the city's new importance, be erected on its site. In 1890 the old hall was purchased for that purpose and, following a competition for architects interested in the project, a young Londoner, Brumwell Thomas, gained the contract. It was his first major undertaking and was to assist in gaining him a Knighthood. The White Linen Hall was demolished and, in 1898 work commenced by H. & J. Martin, a well-known local builders, on the new structure. Officially opened on 1st August 1906 by the Lord Lieutenant (the Earl of Aberdeen) its cost was well over £360,000, a huge amount for that time. The hall has had a primary object of being utilised by the city council for municipal matters, but with its central and open location the building itself and its grounds have afforded space for several of the major public events down the years. The Ulster Covenant of 1912 was signed under the grand dome and, more recently, book-launches, *ceilies* and other less-formal functions have been held inside the Hall whilst its grounds have provided a venue for peace and political rallies.

In the south-west of the grounds was erected in 1925 - 27, to the design of (now knighted) Sir Alfred Brumwell Thomas, the city's Cenotaph and Garden of Remembrance. Scattered elsewhere throughout the gardens are two other memorials to events connected with Belfast or to 'worthies' among its citizens. The Titanic Memorial, which once stood in the middle of Donegall Square North, is now within the railings of the City Hall as is the memorial to the Boer War.

CITY HALL

One has, with rare exceptions, to search today to find relics of Victorian Belfast when once, in the not-so-long-ago, they seemed to be almost everywhere within eye's reach. But with a little diligence, generally with head held high and gaze fixed above ground-floor level, there are gems to be seen. No. 13 Royal Avenue (illustrated) is worth looking at: a stern-looking couple sitting either side of an uninscribed cartouche, probably dating from 1881 when the building was completed as an enhancement to the new Royal Avenue. Magnificently forked-bearded, the gentleman holds what could be a Bible and his female companion what looks like a rock; symbolic of the Rock of Ages? Whatever, this looked far more attractive when it was multi-coloured than it does now with its cheap one-colour covering. Just across the road is the Reform Club (c. 1884) with its fine tiled entrance depicting the Cross of St. Patrick and its Red Hand shield (the right hand, which is proper) surrounded by shamrocks. Tiled floors bearing the company's name were once standard, and this is a classic reminder of that era.

The Linen Hall Library in Donegal Square North is located in what was obviously a linen warehouse; the carving above the entrance denotes that but the Red Hand, emblem of the Ulster linen industry, is wrong as it is the left, rather than the right. The library began in 1788 as the 'Belfast Reading Society', becoming the 'Belfast Society for Promoting Knowledge' four years later and taking its current title from a long residence in the old White Linen Hall sited almost directly opposite. Moving to its present site in 1892, it occupies a building erected to the design of Lanyon, Lynn and Lanyon in 1864 for the Linen merchants, Moore and Weinberg.

Just along from the library, in Wellington Place, can be detected among the shop fronts and advertisments some details from what was once one of Belfast's finest residential thoroughfares. Laid out in the 1790s as part of South Parade it was, by the 1820s, bearing its present name and having its quota of the town's gentry in residence. Included were Thomas Sinclair, the banker Robert Caldwell, the linen merchant William Orr and Staff Surgeon Henry Purdon. Sixty years later, Thomas H. Purdon, also a surgeon, was in occupation of No. 5. Next door, at No. 7 (illustrated) was Robert Henry Sturrock Reade, managing director of the York Street Flax Spinning Company. Reade's home was one of a short terrace built for Adam McClean about 1830 and it and No. 11 retain its once impressive, if now rather dingy, doorcase. Remnants of early Victorian Belfast. George Benn in his 1823 book on Belfast lists Wellington Place as consisting of 8 houses holding 40 males and 66 females, that amazingly high ratio of occupation undoubtedly due to large numbers of servants.

BELFAST DOORWAYS

The Albert Clock, or more correctly The Albert Memorial, is Belfast's equivalent to Italy's famed Leaning Tower of Pisa. It is very obvious that the memorial is out of plumb, noted as far back as 1901, caused by the fact that it was erected on a site reclaimed from the tide and the drying out of the sub-soil is leading to foundation instability.

Albert himself may have been a remote figure to the Belfast folk of his era having only once, with Queen Victoria, visited the town. Nonetheless, when the Prince Consort died in 1861, the town fathers agreed that a display of their loyalty could be no better displayed than by a lasting memorial to him – paid for, of course, by public subscription. A competition was then held which ended in unseemly dispute when the young Newry architect, William J Barre (1830-67) was declared winner. Second were Lanyon, Lynn & Lanyon one of whose principal figures just happened to be a Belfast MP who was in attendance when the decision was made to deprive Barre of his prize and award it to the runners-up. That jobbery was hurriedly reversed when the details became known to a wider audience. It is interesting to note that a similar shambles occurred when Scrabo Tower at Newtownards was being considered: Barre won that competition but Messrs Lanyon who were placed third were given the contract. Ah, for the backing of a secret society!

Barre, who had set up in business in the border town before his 21st birthday, arrived in Belfast just when a massive building programme was being undertaken on both existing and reclaimed land and quickly established himself as an architect of note. Sadly, he died before his 40th year leaving one to wonder just how great he could have become. Anyhow, his Albert Memorial was completed in 1869 in what has been described as in the German-Gothic style and may actually have been to the design of Charles Sherrie, his chief assistant.

Probing almost 30 metres (113 feet) into the air, its four-faced clock can be seen, as intended, over a wide distance. But the grime of industrial Belfast has eroded much of the finery and even the figure of Albert, by S. F. Lynn, younger brother of W. H. Lynn, partner in the Lanyon, Lynn & Lanyon outfit (they had to be rewarded somehow) is showing its age. The removal of the canopy which once gave it some shelter from the elements hasn't helped.

Up until the outbreak of political violence in the 1970s it had long been a tradition of some Belfast folk to welcome in the New Year by gathering at 'the Clock' where, following the normal merriment, bottles and other items were hurled at the monument. High spirits? Or an atavistic response to the anger created when young Barre had, temporarily, lost out to the Lanyon clique?

ALBERT MEMORIAL
(ALBERT CLOCK)

High Street, or Front Street as it was in early times when homes and small shops completed the length between the town church at one end and the castle (where British Home Stores now is), was where Belfast began. The Fearsat river flowed openly down the street, spanned by several small bridges, and the masts of the ships docked at the quays blocked the skyline. Remembrances of those long-ago times are still around us. The bend in Castle Place at the Post Office denotes a curve in the Fearsat's course, and the names of several local thoroughfares remind of the castle. The Internationale shop occupies the site of the Market House wherein the business of the town was conducted and where visiting entertainers performed. But it bore grimmer associations when, in the hot summer of 1798, a gallows was erected beside it from which those found guilty of treason suffered an agonising death, watched in their death throes by the military and citizenry. The most prominent of the victims was Henry Joy McCracken, a member of a well-established family whose only consolation was that his head was not severed from his body as was the custom and carried out on so many others. Their heads were then stuck on spikes on the Market House walls.

After almost 200 years of existence the Market House was pulled away in 1812 and the site developed many times since then. One who had business premises there was Forster Green, a noted member of the local Quaker community who died in 1903 at the advanced age of 88; his home in east Belfast became the Forster Green Hospital. Messrs Woolworth had the Forster Green tea premises levelled, about 1929, to open their first Belfast store with Burton's tailors utilising the corner site until recent times.

The entries linking High Street and Castle Place with, respectively, Ann Street and Rosemary Street have their own stories to tell. Once full of life generated by the families who lived in them, they now serve little purpose than as an access between the major streets. Three, Pottinger's Entry, Wilson's Court and Winecellar Entry each have old established public houses serving the visitor. Crown Entry was where in October 1791 members of the Belfast Presbyterian congregations formed the first branch of the Society of United Irishmen.

Where Castle Place joins Royal Avenue / Donegall Place is known widely as 'Castle Junction' which does not really exist - even if a kiosk there bears the name. It evolved from the early tram service when it was said that every line in the service met at this one spot, forever since known as 'Castle Junction.'

HIGH STREET &
CASTLE PLACE

The 'Morning News' was established by Robert and Daniel Read, its initial issue reaching the streets on July 2nd 1855. Ireland's first penny newspaper, it was an instant success and within a year was selling almost 8,000 copies per issue, 2,000 copies more than the other five Belfast newspapers combined. Though recognised as the Catholic voice, it was much broader and considered liberal in its attitude to political and social issues. The deaths of the Read brothers (Robert 1871, Daniel 1881) led to the paper's acquisition by Edmund Dwyer Gray, owner of the 'Freeman's Journal' in Dublin, and it remained with the Gray family until taken over by the 'Irish News' ten years later.

The repercussions of the Charles Stewart Parnell liaison with Kathleen O'Shea, wife of Capt. William O'Shea, were felt in Belfast as elsewhere throughout Ireland. The County Wicklow landlord and leader of the Irish Home Rule party had been lauded as another Daniel O'Connell, but in the moral climate of the time his love for another man's wife stunned and horrified society not, it should be noted, that some members of his party and others in a wider sphere had not been aware of what had been going on. In Belfast effects were profound.

The Catholic hierarchy were scandalised, and when the 'Morning News' refused to continue with its anti-Parnell stance there was seen a necessity to publish a news sheet which would. Dr. Patrick McAllister, Bishop of Down and Connor, and others, gathered funds and support for a new paper: on 15th August 1891 the first 'Irish News' appeared.

Faced by such a determined and powerful opposition it was only a matter of time before the 'Morning News' succumbed and on 29th August 1892 the 'Irish News' appeared with the sub-title of 'Belfast Morning News'. The new paper was strongly Nationalist, and perhaps even more strongly Catholic, in its outlook, the latter somewhat alleviated when Joe Devlin, M.P. and his United League gained control in 1905, a control held until Devlin's death in 1934. Dr. Daniel McSparran from the Antrim Glens succeeded Devlin as chairman, thus substantiating the first of the family 'dynasties' to control the 'Irish News'. McSparran was followed by his son, also Dr. Daniel, but with his tragic death in a car accident in May 1981 (his sister Mary, company secretary, was also killed) James J. Fitzpatrick, whose family had been directors since the late 1930s, took control in 1983.

Originally sited a couple of doors closer to York Street, the 'Irish News' moved into its current premises in 1905 to a new building designed by J. J. McDonnell. This was the site of a cotton-spinning factory owned by John McCracken, member of a well-known local family.

THE IRISH NEWS

This was, or was close to, the site of the ancient 'Chapel of the Ford' the earliest known place of worship in what is now Belfast city centre. In time, that little chapel was removed and a much larger church erected with that church being a scene of scandal to the Belfast folk of the 1640s. Oliver Cromwell, learning that Belfast was holding out for the King, dispatched Colonel Robert Venables and a troop of military to bring the surly Belfast Royalists to heel and, after taking the town with but a listless defensive struggle, the Colonel converted the church into a citadel. Cromwell himself never was to see what his emissary had done, though one wonders whether it would have drawn his praise or his anger.

That old church was demolished in 1774 and the present St. George's opened for worship on 16th June 1816, the architect being John Bowden of Dublin. The portico, however, came from another source having been planned for the unfinished home of the Earl Bishop of Derry, Ballyscullion House near Castledawson. The portico was dismantled, loaded into lighters and floated across Lough Neagh and down the Lagan Canal into Belfast. Whilst constructing the new St. George's, opportunity was taken to remove the old town graveyard which surrounded the old church where lay the remains of so many once prominent townites ; the Pottingers of nearby Pottinger's Entry and Mountpottinger in Ballymacarrett, the McCrackens and David Manson the town's favourite educationalist.

From near Larne, Manson arrived in Belfast as a brewer but quickly turned to teaching when finding brewing a too competitive occupation. His schoolhouse was in lower Donegall Street and there he taught by methods far advanced of his time. Punishment was out and the children were encouraged to read the daily newspapers and generally made aware of their contribution to society. So much was Manson respected that he was given a night funeral at which the mourners carried candles and torches, the ultimate accolade at that time.

The resurrected St. George's sat back only a short distance from the town dock and, perhaps, the rattle of ships' spars and the creaking of timbers as they rubbed against the quay walls, disturbed the good burgesses at their prayers. But after prayer some may well have acquainted themselves with the ships' crews and learned of lands and customs beyond the waters of Belfast Lough. There is still, of an evening, a peacefulness in this part of old Belfast - harking back to a different era.

ST. GEORGE'S CHURCH

In political terms the Ulster Hall is perhaps more noted for the meeting that did not take place within its walls than any that have. Back in 1912, during the heat generated by the Home Rule crisis Winston Churchill, then in favour of self-government in Ireland, was due to address his followers in the Bedford Street hall. But Unionists had booked the venue the previous evening and refused to leave when called upon to do so, forcing Churchill and company to make do with Celtic Park which was hastily placed at their disposal. Down the years since, many lesser-known mortals have made the old building rock with tirades of political invective, rallying party members to greater effort for whatever cause.

There have been the Gospel preachers and, as intended when the hall was first mooted, the musical entertainers, both classical and pop, who have drawn the crowds. A hall meant for culture, enlightenment and for the betterment of the citizens of Belfast was, contrary to expectations, filled more often by crowds more interested in witnessing two males battering the daylights out of each other than in any broadening of academic knowledge. Boxing had been first staged there over a century ago when the great John L. Sullivan, idol of Irish-America and of the Irish at home, gave an exhibition of the 'Noble Art' with a sparring partner. Admission was not cheap, 5 shillings (25p) for orchestra chairs, 3 shillings reserved seats, 2 shillings balcony and unreserved 1 shilling. Expensive enough for the 1880s. But the hall was packed - *to suffocation* as one report had it - leading one to conclude that not all in attendance belonged to the 'poorer classes.'

Boxing, amateur and professional, was only a sporadic item on the Ulster Hall calendar until the close-by 'Chapel Fields' were ordered to finish in 1939 and the legendary 'Ma' Copley transferred her business to the Ulster Hall. With support equal to that found anywhere in these islands she carried on for some years to be succeeded by brothers John and George Connell. Twice weekly, Wednesday and Saturday, the fans trekked to Bedford Street until the economic impositions of the mid-1950s led to a cut-back in the game and a receding to its pre-'Ma' Copley level.

W. J. Barre, whose input to Belfast's architecture included Bryson House next door to the Ulster Hall, supervised building of the hall from 1859 until its official opening in May 1862. Large enough to accommodate 250 performers and a 2000 strong audience, it was enhanced by a magnificent organ donated by the Mulhollands of York Street Flax Spinning Company, an appropriate gesture considering that this is 'Linenapolis' where the product of the Mulholland mill was given its finishing touches.

THE ULSTER HALL

Waddell Cunningham is a name which means little to the Belfastian of today, but in the last half of the 18th century he was believed the wealthiest man in the town. How he gained his wealth remains a mystery, though the story that he was eager to engage his fellow merchants in the odious slave trade may be a clue. His offer of investment was rightly spurned by those to whom it was made, leaving it to the 'gentry' of Bristol and Liverpool to enrich themselves on the tears, blood and sweat of human beings. But Waddell was not all bad - he was a founder of the Irish Volunteers who became the vanguard for reform in his time. And when in 1784 Belfast's first Catholic church since the Reformation, St. Mary's in Crooked (now Chapel) Lane was opened he played his part in mustering his men as Guard of Honour for Fr. Hugh O'Donnell. Interestingly, that little church was only yards from Cunningham's home which was somewhere about the site of the Tesco store. He died in 1797 thus evading the events of the following year which convulsed Antrim and Down, but some years earlier his home had been threatened by the agrarian Hearts of Steel who stormed Belfast barracks and then turned on Cunningham when one of their men had been, unjustly in their eyes, imprisoned. Stirring times, and Waddell, in a manner, may have been better pleased when his days ended and he found repose in his grand mausoleum in Knockbreda churchyard.

The Catholic Church came into possession of the Cunningham home and established their Belfast Catholic Institute, but whether in the former dwelling or in a new building remains unclear. In 1875, to the rear of the Institute, was erected St. Mary's Hall which held Diocesan offices and a large auditorium in which entertainments took place until some years prior to its demolition in 1989. But before the hall had been built, the Catholic Institute had gone and in replacement rose the splendid Provincial Bank to the plans of W. J. Barre. Unfortunately, Barre died in 1867 and the bank's completion, deviating from his designs, was carried out by Turner and Williamson. Finished in 1869 it holds to the street line of the old Hercules Place and is the sole remainder of the period prior to Hercules Place and Street being levelled to make way for Royal Avenue.

Across Bank Street (so appropriately named, either from being a bank of the Fearsat River or from the Commercial Banks on its banks!) was another and earlier financial enterprise, a short-lived bank in which Waddell Cunningham appears to have been a partner. Primark occupy that site whilst the Provincial Bank became the Allied Irish Bank and ultimately Tesco. The latter have sympathetically treated what is an outstanding building and a visit to the former banking hall conveys its grandeur.

No. 2 ROYAL AVENUE

Right up through the 1950s this was the foremost entertainments area of Belfast as nearby could be found three of the city's principal cinemas - Imperial, Royal Cinema and Classic - and the lively Empire Theatre which staged plays, held concerts and whatever it believed would draw an audience. There were also several popular eating houses and public houses, of which the renowned Mooney's is possibly best remembered. Add to those regular commercial offerings the numerous street buskers who, mostly badly out of tune and lacking any kind of flair, cadged for a few pennies from those in the seemingly interminable queues. Standard for the times, they were at their worst on Fridays and Saturdays with the Imperial adding more torture as it had a double queueing system: line up outside for a ticket at the inside kiosk and then again beyond the kiosk before being admitted to the auditorium. They have all gone, the Imperial was first, in 1959, with the Royal Cinema and Classic two years later. The Empire also shut in 1961 following a century of theatrics performed on some two or three stages on the site.

One of Belfast's earliest theatres had been opened in 1793 where the Imperial was later built making this the longest continuous site for amusement in the city. To that old Theatre Royal came Mrs Sarah Siddons, Charles Kemble, Edmund Kean and William Macready, all celebrated in their day. And, no doubt, the local taverns and hotels also had entertainments for guest and casual visitor alike. We do know that in Cornmarket there was for some years in the 1830s the New Harmonic Saloon: singing public houses, then as now, were well patronised. For those desirous of more intellectual stimuli it was necessary to move outside the bounds of Cornmarket to partake of what was on offer at the Belfast Harp Society, the Natural History & Philosophical Society, the Belfast Naturalists' Field Club, the Belfast Philharmonic Society, the Belfast & North of Ireland Ornithological Society or the North of Ireland International Dog Show Society, some of which are still in existence. For the more wealthy there were several men's clubs - the Northern, the Ulster, the Union - plus yacht and cricket organisations; a wide selection. Except for the Bandstand, Arthur Square/Cornmarket has little in the way of entertainment to offer nowadays. But the band stage is a venue for musical and singing groups and to pressure groups protesting about old-age pensions or such social items. A final note. The large structure behind the Band Stand is the Masonic Buildings, erected 1869 to the design of Charles Lanyon, himself a prominent member. Another place of amusement in its own manner.

BANDSTAND, CORNMARKET

Hidden away, somewhat off the normal tourist trail, is what can justifiably be argued is Belfast's rarest gem, the Catholic church of St. Malachy in the upper markets district of the city. Only a few minutes stroll from the rear of the City Hall, it has been described by one commentator as *"a wedding cake turned inside out."* And that refers only to the ceiling:– the pulpit, the altar and the fine three-sided balcony draws the eye to an accumulation of man-made beauty rarely encountered in a small parish church.

But this, apparently, was not intended always to remain a simple parish church as there was a grander idea of making it the Cathedral for the Diocese of Down and Connor. The area was then open country, and a sign of the better days then pertaining is the knowledge that the owner of the land, Adam McClean, a Presbyterian, donated the site to Hugh Magill *'in trust for the Catholics of Belfast'*. Mr Magill was acting on behalf of the Catholic Bishop and, on 3rd November 1841, the foundation stone was laid. The church was opened in December 1844, its architect being Thomas Jackson. But though Jackson was one of the town's senior architects the *'pièce de résistance'* of the church is the interior decoration. The altar is known to be the work of Felix Piccioni one of the earliest of the Italian community to practice in Belfast.

With its twin turrets and castellated roofline and the Diocesan memorials on shields above the main entrance, the best view of St. Malachy's is from Clarence Street, particularly on an evening when the sun is still bright and casting side shadows. But what is not commonly known is that once the church bore a high spire which had to be taken down to appease Messrs Dunville's who had a warehouse just across the street. It seems that the whisky company complained that the church bells when ringing were casting vibrations which prevented the whisky maturing! The spire was removed in 1913 and one presumes that the Dunville product ripened safely thereafter. Yet in a city which boasts so much of its religiosity it is surely odd that, if the above story is true, the profits of a whisky distiller should take precedence over a people's call to worship.

As the area developed with warehouses the church lost its rural aspect and, no doubt, the thoughts of it becoming the Diocesan Cathedral lessened. Thankfully it remains, much as it was designed, to remind us of the superb craftsmanship which went into its completion.

ST. MALACHY'S CHURCH

Not so long ago the Donegall Quay loçale could well have been classed as the busiest area within the limits of Belfast. The nightly and, when occasion demanded, the daily cross-channel vessels left here for ports in England and Scotland, each carrying their passengers and cargo. The nearby docks, Clarendon and York, filled and disgorged their freights, at all times of day and night as necessity required. Ships' repairs were carried out, annual Lloyd's surveys seen to, supplies obtained from ship chandlers and purveyors of whatever else was necessary. This was, in essence, the Port of Belfast. It was only across the way in Corporation Square that the Scotsman, William Ritchie, had set up the town's initial shipbuilding company away back in 1791. At that time, Donegall Quay was still subject to the tidal waters of Belfast Lough and open marsh land stretched beyond Ritchie's up to Cave Hill with only the odd farm dotted here and there.

As sea-going trade moved from its original location at the foot of the High Street on to land reclaimed from the Lough, Donegall Quay and the facing Queen's Quay became almost incessantly crowded with shipping and horses and carts and the varying passenger-carrying cabs rattled over the Mourne granite square-setts which formed the cover for most of Belfast's roads. Exciting and challenging, the first face of a world-renowned seaport. On the opposite shore and looking down lough, the great gantries of Harland & Wolff created a spider's web pattern as they clustered round the various graving docks. There was a train here, partly under street level, linking the now-gone County Down railway at Queen's Quay with the former L. M. S. in York Street. A section of the rail tracks can still be seen in Princess Dock Street where wagons rattled past those at service in St. Joseph's Church.

Thus it was, right up through the 1950s when, as the poet put it 'all was changed'. Shipping berths moved further out into the Lough, the cross-channel passenger service all but ceased, leaving the hustle and bustle of Donegall Quay hushed. No more dockers assembling in their hundreds for daily work; no more families and individuals boarding ship for employment or holiday; no trains ran; and Billy the trace-horse who assisted loaded carts take the small, sharp incline to Queen's Bridge was retired to a less stressful life. But Tedford's remains as a relic of those days, a lovely little creation by Alexander McAllister which has been on this spot since 1855. Its external decoration reveals its nautical connection, even if its original use in the days of sail and steam lies in the dreams of Belfast.

TEDFORD'S CHANDLERY

THE PEOPLE OF THE CITY

In comparison with many other urban settlements in Ireland, Belfast is modern. Its earliest mention by the annalists is for the year 665 when a battle was recorded as occurring at the Fearsat between the Ulidians and the mysterious Cruithne. It is then almost half a millennium before the place is again considered worthy of mention when the Anglo-Norman, John de Courcy, invaded Ulster. His incursion began in 1177 and over the next decade and a half the accounts are of battles and struggles between the various factions each keen to hold possession of the ancient fording place as it enabled a more direct route of passage from strongholds at Downpatrick and Dundrum in County Down to Carrickfergus in Antrim. Earlier, the Vikings had had some involvement in the area, though to what extent is still open to conjecture. It was their drive which had created the impetus for the

growth of such as Dublin and Waterford and many of the place names on the east coast of Ireland tell of their presence; from the likes of Howth and Lambey in the Dublin locale to Carlingford and Strangford in, respectively, Louth and Down. In the immediate Belfast region the remains of the round tower at Drumbo, just outside the south-eastern limits of the city, suggest that the men from the northern lands had considered this old monastic site worthy of their attention. The Drumbo monastery is reputed to date from Patrician times, though the earliest references to a church in what was to become Belfast, is several centuries later, in 1306. Shankill and the 'Chapel of the Ford' are both listed but both, particularly Shankill, were probably much older - certainly pre-Norman.

At some stage a fortification had been

erected to command the ford at Belfast, presumably Norman, though perhaps laid on an earlier structure. In the numerous struggles for local and wider supremacy which dominates medieval history, Antrim and Down bore their share of conflict. In 1315 the Ulster native chieftains invited Robert Bruce of Scotland to come to their aid against what was seen as a joint enemy but the Scottish king, unable to cross over himself, sent his brother, Edward, in his stead. During May, Edward landed at Larne and was proclaimed 'King of Ireland.' Of his adventures in Ireland the poet, Edmund Spencer, wrote that he (Bruce)

"wasted Belfast, Greencastle, Kells, Belturbet, Castletown, Newtown, and many other very good towns and strongholds."

Spencer was writing in 1595, long after the events allegedly occurred, and whether Belfast as early as 1315 could be honestly described as a 'very good town' is open to question. Bruce's campaign came to an end in 1318 when at Faughart, just north of Dundalk, he was slain when his combined Scots and Irish army was defeated by a combination of Anglo-Irish under command of John de Bermingham of Thethmoy.

The horrors of war had devastated east Ulster and down into Munster with, in the former area, the Anglo-Norman de Burgo family regaining control. But their hold was short-lived as in 1333 William de Burgo, the 21 year old Earl of Ulster, was killed at Skegoniel, about a mile to the north of the castle at Belfast. He was, the story tells, on his way to Carrickfergus for Sunday Mass and his death so enraged the Anglo-Irish that they asserted revenge by seizing all whom they suspected of complicity in the affair, slaughtering some 300.

The death of de Burgo broke, more-or-less, the power of the Anglo-Normans in the region as the O'Neills, moving eastwards from their strongholds around Tullaghoge in County Tyrone, came to occupy the lower reaches of the Lagan Valley. Belfast Castle was a major prize and over the next couple of centuries it passed through various hands. In 1476 the O'Neills are noted as demolishing it, but it was apparently rebuilt as Hugh Roe O'Donnell (the O'Donnells being traditional foes of the O'Neills) captured it in 1489. Fourteen years later, Garret Mor Fitzgerald, the 'great' Earl of Kildare, destroyed the castle and, following its reconstruction, was back again in 1512 to once again raze it. In another journey north, Garret Og Fitzgerald, son of Garret Mor, conquered, and in a letter to Henry VIII, boasted that he had taken the castle from Hugh O'Neill (Hew McNeile, as he described him) and had burned 24 miles of the land around. Another O'Neill, Conn, First Earl of Tyrone, then entered the picture in this confusing period of Belfast's, and Ireland's history. Ulster was in continuous

revolt, and though the Anglo-Normans and the succeeding English were able to maintain their hold on Carrickfergus and other coastal forts their hold was constantly being challenged by the native people.

That Conn O'Neill had accepted his Earldom from Henry VIII never prevented many of the O'Neill clan displaying their unwillingness to accept loss of their lands and rights. But an uneasy peace slowly settled over Ulster and, in the Belfast district, the Clandeboye (from Clann Aodha Buidhe, meaning family of Yellow-haired Hugh) O'Neills appeared reasonably content with their lot. In 1553 Hugh O'Neill was noted as having:-

"two castles, one called Bealefarst, an old castle standing upon a ford that leadeth from Ards to Clanneboye, which being well repaired, being now broken, would be a good defence between the woods and Knockfergus [Carrickfergus]. *The other,*

called Castellrioughe [Castlereagh]*, is four miles from Bealefarst, and standeth upon the plain in the midst of the woods of the Dufferin."*

It is the latter which is most associated with the O'Neill occupation of Belfast.

That letter had been written by Sir Thomas Cusack, then Lord Chancellor, and indicates that the Crown recognised the O'Neill title to both castles. But times were still unsettled and fourteen years on, William Piers and Nicholas Malbie, military officers in Belfast, informed Queen Elizabeth that:-

"the rest of the country between this and the English pale [i.e between Belfast and north of Dundalk] *are in good quietness. We have fortified Belfast and have placed their fifteen horsemen so that in this town we live as quietly as Dublin."*

But they did have a complaint, the quality of the local beer was poor and they *"drunk water rather than to stand in the danger of ... infection."*!

The Elizabethan era injected a new dimension to the Anglo-Irish situation. The Old English in Ireland were, and many were to remain, Catholics, and in several instances were known to be 'more Irish than the Irish' whilst the new settlers and planters were of the reformed faiths. Now, faced with ancient struggle for land and political rights, was added an intent to control the religious soul. It was to be some time yet before full penal restrictions were to be imposed on Catholics, Presbyterians and other dissenters, but the groundwork was being laid. In 1573 the Queen granted Walter Devereux, Earl of Essex, much of the county of Antrim, including *'the river of Belfast'*. The term *'river'* surely indicates just how little Belfast was at that period. This grant to Essex coincided or superseded a grant of much of County Down and Belfast to Sir Thomas Smith, though it was Essex who seemingly was superior. It led to a battle with Sir Brian O'Neill near the ford shortly afterwards. The protagonists were restored to peace, a peace shattered with what is the greatest act of treachery ever to darken the memory of Belfast Castle.

O'Neill invited Essex and his men to a feast at the castle, and after three days of merriment Essex ordered his men to seize his host and retainers, putting some 150 to immediate death and sending Brian, his wife and brother to Dublin where they were hung, drawn and quartered. The O'Neills, however, still held Castlereagh with, in the meantime, Essex recording his

"resolve not to build but at one place ; namely Belfast; and that of littel charge; a small towns there will keeps the passage. reliefe Knockfergus [Carrickfergus] *with wood, and horsemen being laid there shall command the plains of clandeboye, and with footemen may kepe the passage open between that and the Newrie* [Newry]...*"*

His intentions were forestalled by his death the following year.

Due, no doubt, to the abundant woods hereabout this was an ideal place at which to build ships and to Sir John Perret, Lord Deputy, goes the honour of singling out Belfast for that purpose. That was in 1584, but there was to be much blood spilt and horrors committed before ship building came to pass. Belfast Castle was taken by Shane McBryan in 1597, but soon afterwards the first of the Chichesters, Sir John, repossessed it. Following an argument with the McDonnells of north Antrim at Altfracken, near Ballycarry, Chichester was killed before the year was out and Sir Ralph Lane took charge of Belfast, but in 1599 was appointed to the region Sir Arthur Chichester, brother to the slain Sir John.

The People

The Chichesters were from Devonshire and Arthur had had to flee England due to having waylaid the Queen's tax-gatherer which was a capital offence. Making amends for his crime he was sent to Ireland and there his cruelty was profound. He was to write that;

"I spayre neither house, corne, nor creature ... sparing none of what quality, age, or sex soever; besides many burned to death, we kill man, woman, child, horse beast, and whatsoever we find."

This was, in his own words, the man credited with founding Belfast; what he couldn't kill with the sword he destroyed through starvation and pestilence. It was, indeed, a period of great savagery and Chichester, in appreciation of his work, was granted the *"appurtenants and hereditaments, spiritual and temporal"* of the castle of Belfast in 1603, was made Lord Deputy of Ireland in 1604, supervised the plantation of Ulster in 1607 and was created Baron Chichester of Belfast in 1612.

In 1613, he obtained for Belfast his first Charter of Incorporation which gave it the right to have its own governing council of a sovereign and twelve burgesses, in modern terms, a mayor and 12 councillors. But, whilst he lived, those positions were all in the power of Arthur Chichester to bestow, and that undemocratic nepotism was to be adhered to, with but little alteration, until 1842 when the first properly elected council for the town was chosen.

The O'Neill stronghold at Castlereagh fell, by stratagem, to Chichester and to the Montgomerys, later with associations with the Ards; James Hamilton, afterwards Lord Viscount Clandeboye, was also involved. Thus the O'Neill hold on Belfast was ended. Arthur Chichester died in 1625 and by then the family grasp was solid. A nephew, Colonel Arthur Chichester was created Earl

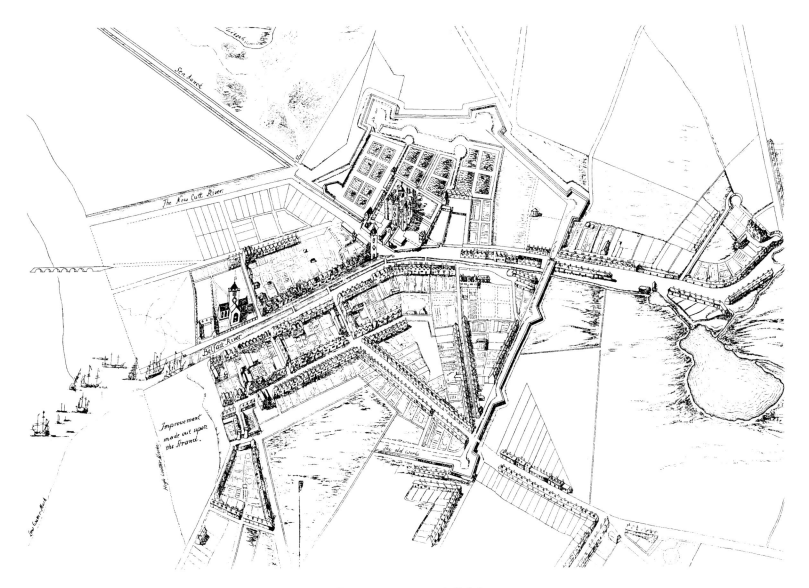

The New Cutt River

Sea bank

Belfast River

Improvement made out upon the Strand.

BELFAST C. 1665
(MAP EXTRACT REPRODUCED COURTESY LINEN HALL LIBRARY)

THE PEOPLE

Donegall (from land held on the Inishowen Peninsula) in 1647 and so both names, Chichester and Donegall, are today found naming thoroughfares throughout the city.

Belfast with its Charter was one of the so-called 'Rotten Boroughs' of King James I, created, it was claimed, by that monarch to strengthen his hold on the throne. Whatever, it was dominated by its castle which, as outlined above, had often been wrecked and rebuilt. The final edifice was, as shown in old illustrations, much more of a fortified residence than any true fortress. It was accidentally burned down in 1708, ending the Chichester / Donegall residence in the town for a century. The town itself was described by a visitor, Torevin de Rocheford, in 1672 as being;-

"situate on a river at the bottom of a gulf where barks and vessels anchor on account of the security and goodness of the port; wherefore several merchants live here who trade to Scotland and England, wither they transport the superfluities of this country ... Here is a very fine castle and two or three large and straight streets, as in a new-built town."

An early comment of interest. The Donegalls, with their castle burnt down, transported themselves back to England and were to be absentee landlords throughout the 18th century.

To revert back a bit. The previous hundred years had witnessed continued disturbances in Ireland, notably with the wars of the 1640s and that of the 1689-90 period. Belfast avoided any direct involvements in either set of conflicts though it did have experience of both. In the battle between Crown and Parliament which was causing problems in England and the strife in Ireland when the native Irish supported by some of the Old English were opposing England's claim to Ireland, General Robert

Munro arrived at Carrickfergus in April 1642 with 2,500 men in aid of the Lords Chichester, Clandeboye and Ards. The demand by the Earl of Leven, who had followed Munro with reinforcements, that all forces under his command, English and Scots, should subscribe to the Church of Scotland Covenant was opposed by Chichester and others. A rampart had been constructed round the town to hold back any attempt by the rebellious Irish to take Belfast and this, it was believed, would also hold back Munro should he attempt to invade. But the Scotsman easily walked in when, conveniently, the north gate was left open for his entry.

Not quite as lucky was Colonel Robert Venables in the June of seven years later who under orders from his superior Oliver Cromwell who had learned that Belfast was holding out for the monarchy, arrived to put the place under republican rule. But the resistance offered was quite brief and did provide an irony in that a rampart built to hold back the native Irish was only ever defended to repel the invading English! Cromwell himself never came to Belfast and that, knowing of his propensity to slaughter garrisons elsewhere, must be considered a stroke of fortune. And when, at the century's end, the struggles culminating at the Battle of the Boyne and Siege of Limerick, the only connection Belfast had was that William, on his way to the Boyne, stayed for a couple of days in the castle.

The 1700s was basically a period of consolidation, when the town gradually grew in size and population as commerce was extended with new docks and quays being provided to enable larger vessels to load and unload right in the High Street. There was the occasional scare such as when riots occasioned by the potato failure erupted in 1756 and when, four years later, word was received from Carrickfergus that the French-Irish privateer, Monsieur Thurot,

The People

had taken Carrick and was threatening Belfast. A volunteer defensive force was hastily assembled, but wasn't needed as Thurot stayed content with his booty elsewhere.

By mid-century the population had grown to around 8,000 and much of the central town as it is now had taken shape. As the years went to century's end, cotton manufacturing, rope-making and ship-building were established, a sure signal that Belfast was leaving behind its image as a purely marketing town. With confidence engendered by business success, went hand in glove a radicalism which was prepared to challenge the Irish government in Dublin and the more powerful government in London, demanding full economic and religious rights for all the people of Ireland.

The town was predominately Presbyterian in religious concept and it was principally their voice which barked loudest. The war in the American colonies was heavily backed by emigrant Presbyterians from counties Antrim and Down who helped form a militant force described as being *'the backbone of Washington's army'*. With regular troops being shipped out to defend the colonies, a volunteer force was raised in Ireland in case of French invasion but that new force, in Belfast and its hinterlands, became quite radical in asserting demands similar to those raised by their relatives in the New World. They wanted repeal of all obnoxious legalisation regarding taxes, a fair representation in parliament and full religious liberties for all. The fall of the Bastille in Paris was greatly welcomed and twice the Volunteers paraded in the streets of Belfast to commemorate the event with, on the second occasion, a banquet in the White Linen Hall. The Belfast Volunteer units were the first in Ireland to admit Catholics to their ranks and, with the backing of their townsfolk, were most strident in demanding Catholic Emancipation. They displayed

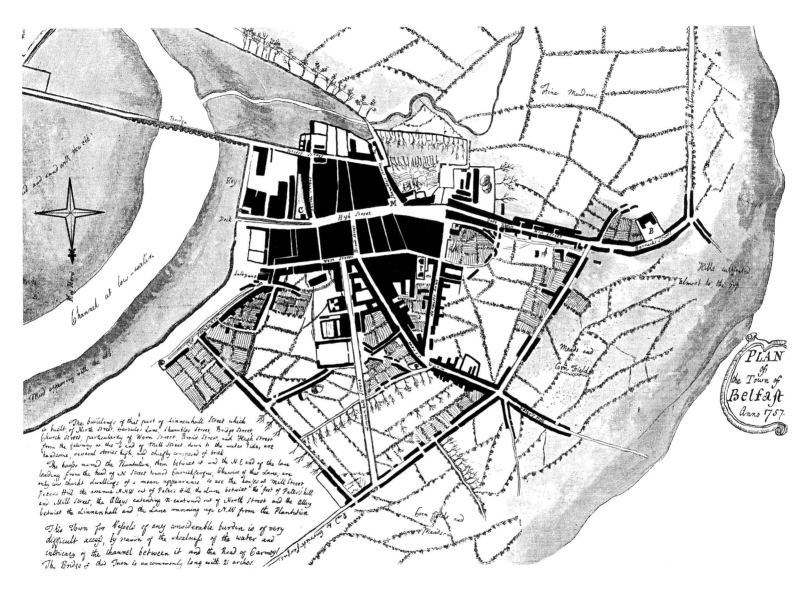

BELFAST C. 1757

(MAP EXTRACT REPRODUCED COURTESY LINEN HALL LIBRARY)

THE PEOPLE

their liberality by subscribing heavily to the erecting of St. Mary's church, the first Catholic church in Belfast since the Reformation, providing a guard of honour for Fr. Hugh O'Donnell at its opening and attending at his opening Mass. The government, unable to resist such open defiance due to its military force being otherwise engaged, conceded many of the demands made but, when the American war ended and the danger from France abated, their attitude hardened considerably.

The Volunteers were stood down, but by then a newer, even more radical grouping, had been formed, the Society of United Irishmen. Again it was Presbyterian, and their original meeting in October 1791 was in Crown Entry off the High Street. They were not so easily bought or frightened off. The government, however, through its agents within the movement knew much of what was going on and proceeded to flood Belfast, and other areas in Ireland believed

dangerous by this new movement, with soldiers and militia. The northern town, believed the most radical in the British Isles, had special attention paid to it as the troops were given free rein and encouraged to frighten the people into subjection or into premature rebellion.

Monsieur de Latocnaye, a French Royalist who would have had little time or sympathy for revolutionists, has left an account of how Belfast was at that time. It was on a return visit he wrote:-

"The people of this town who were represented some time ago as about to rise, appeared now in a sort of stupor hardly indistinguishable from fear. In the evening the town was illuminated [for the King's birthday] *and the soldiers ran through the streets armed with sticks, breaking the windows of these who had not lit up their houses, and of a great number who had done so. They went into all sorts of holes and corners*

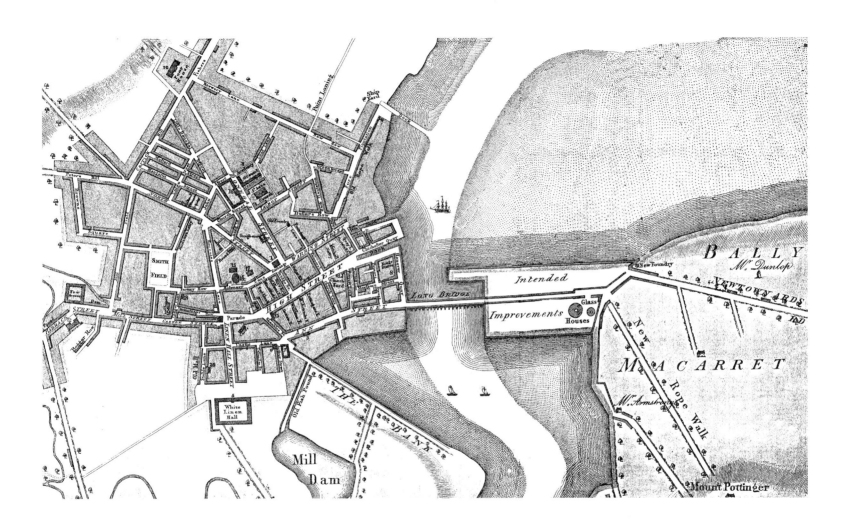

Belfast c. 1791

(Map extract reproduced courtesy Linen Hall Library)

THE PEOPLE

breaking back-windows and the fanlights of doors. They seized their officers and bore them, in turn, on their shoulders through the streets. The yells, coming from the soldiers, and the huzzas were simply terrible. ... I was much surprised to see the soldiers had taken the trouble to break windows as far as two or three miles from the town."

Insurrection did take place, beginning in the southern counties and in the north, finally, on June 7th with an attack on Antrim town. But without French assistance there was simply no way a poorly-armed untrained force could win the day. Courage and idealism could win battles but never the war. And so it proved, with the skilled troops backed by a heavily-armed militia over-powering the peasant army, and the gallows in the High Street of Belfast carried its share of grisly evidence. Decapitation followed the hangings with the heads of the victims being spiked on the Market House as a warning to all. In a small town, such as Belfast then was, where almost everyone knew each other, the effects must have been horrific.

But the liberalism of the people was not yet quenched. The calls for Catholic Emancipation continued and only ended when that measure was finally ensured in 1829. The town's second Catholic church, St. Patrick's in Donegall Street, owed a debt to the Protestant people who gave money towards its building. Ironically, one of those who donated cash (one hundred guineas, quite a substantial amount at that time) was Lord Castlereagh who bore much responsibly in quelling the 1798 Rebellion. Still, the signs of religious discord were becoming evident as people flocking into the growing industrial capital of Ireland brought with them the religious antagonisms of the rural districts. It was an explosive mix; competition for jobs (needed to ensure some standard of living) combined with long-established sectarian bitterness. Yet Belfast continued its inexorable growth, from some 20,000 inhabitants at the start of the century to almost 400,000 at its end: the fastest growing urban centre in these islands.

William Ritchie had brought over his ship-building skills in 1791, but his efforts were surpassed by Edward Harland, a Yorkshireman, who arrived during the 1850s. Harland, with the German, Gustav Wilhelm Wolff, was to develop in Belfast one of the world's greatest shipyards. Then there was the development of the linen trade, the rope-making works, the aerated-water companies and Gallaher's tobacco company, all contributing to make Belfast one of the greatest industrial cities the world had ever seen.

These main industries led to jobs in heavy engineering, in the building trades and in the retail outlets causing the old Belfast to become only the centre of a booming metropolis. Sedate residential quarters converted to shopping and factories and mills encroached on what, not too long before, had been green fields on the town's suburbs.

Land, once under the tidal waters of Belfast Lough and the River Lagan, was reclaimed for more town centre expansion. The old docks in the High Street were removed as newer and better quays were constructed beside the reclaimed ground. To enable larger shipping to reach Belfast the bottom of the Lough was dredged to form what became the Victoria Channel, and Queen Victoria with her consort, Albert, made her only ever visit to the town in 1849 to officially open it. The same year, the Queens College, one of three such institutions in Ireland admitted its first students; it later became The Queen's University of Belfast. A new custom house was completed in 1857, with a new bridge spanning the Lagan to make easier the transfer of people and goods between

THE PEOPLE

Antrim and Down. The population kept on growing necessitating more and more housing, more schools, more churches, more places of entertainment. There were, of course, lulls in this expansion as commercial events in the outer world affected industry in Belfast. Ireland, with its relatively small population overall, required access to a larger market for its products and it was fortunate that in Belfast there was not only the expertise to make the goods but the contacts to whom to sell them.

But there was a continuous downside to all this industrial and commercial success. Religious differences were regularly raising their discords and too often the town, (city from 1888), was racked with bitterness. There was dispute within several of the main churches in individual interpretation of the Bible with clergy such as Dr. Henry Cooke disputing Presbyterianism with Dr. Henry Montgomery. The Church of Ireland, for long the State Church, was disestablished in 1869. The establishing of the three Queen's Colleges, in Belfast, Cork and Galway, had brought out the ire of Cardinal Paul Cullen, a senior Catholic ecclesiastical, to what were being described as "Godless Colleges" due to their lack of direct church involvement. All of those internal church arguments were grist to the mills of the bigots. And there were the ongoing political arguments.

The appearance of Daniel O'Connell in Belfast led to street riots even though he had forcefully condemned the use of violence in any striving to alter the political connection between Ireland and Britain. When rumours of local involvement with the 1860s Fenian Movement were mooted in the town, the Belfast Catholic Clergy read a statement from their pulpits condemning it. The earlier Young Ireland Rebellion was of limited duration and seemingly had no, or little, affect on the northern town. But the Irish Republican brotherhood (the I.R.B.) emerging from the Fenians had some

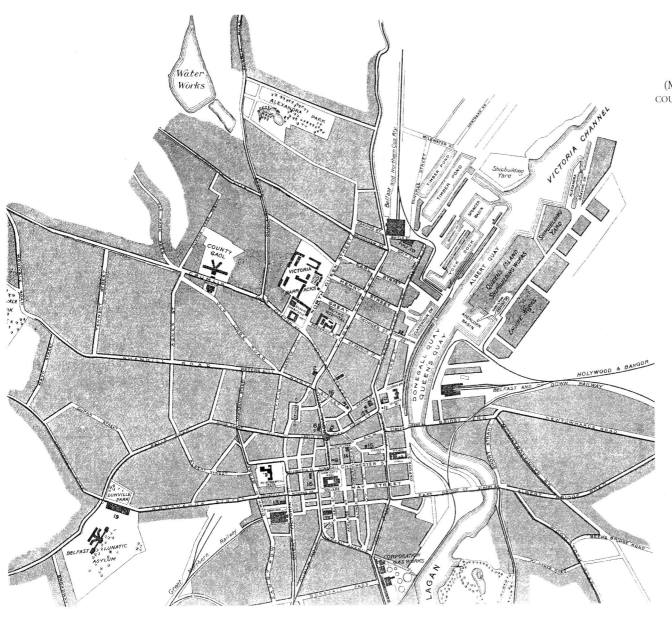

BELFAST
C. 1906
(MAP EXTRACT REPRODUCED
COURTESY LINEN HALL LIBRARY)

THE PEOPLE

support, though the bulk of local Nationalism was intentionally peaceful. On the opposing side was the quasi-religious Orange Order and, later, the Ulster Volunteer Force, both with considerable support in Belfast. The Home Rule debates at Westminster were eagerly followed in the local press and street rioting became a constant cause of alarm. The outbreak of war in Europe in 1914 drew some of the sting from the argument as huge numbers of U.V.F. members enlisted in the Crown forces. They were joined by equally large numbers of local Catholics who supported the Nationalist Party's plea for recruitment. War's end and the setting up of the two states in Ireland, brought intensive rioting to the streets of Belfast, with a, thankfully short-lived, spasm occurring in 1935. Then there were the more current troubles which resurrected old hatreds and animosities.

But Belfast had much more to offer its citizens and its visitors than dour deeds.

There was, and is, humour and entertainment and a natural friendliness behind it all.

The city is again undergoing much architectural change with most of its manufacturing capacity now lodged in the suburbs or adjacent council areas such as Castlereagh and Newtownabbey. The old traditional industries are all but gone; linen has become a luxury, modern shipbuilding techniques have drastically reduced manpower, imports and competition from overseas, plus local manufacturing in former market countries has reduced Belfast sales. This is the modern world into which all countries and cities must be able to fit.

Due to steady movement since the 1960s out of the older city areas to more modern housing on the suburbs or nearby commuter towns, the population of Belfast has dropped to some 280,000. That has meant a closure of several schools, whilst the introduction of the supermarket has led to most of the older-established retailers selling out. That in turn has maybe led to a loss of character within the older, familiar inner-city areas. It is a problem facing all cities and one for which an adequate and definite policy has not yet been found. But the city which grew from a simple ford on a sandy river-side, remains Belfast.

SELECT BIBLIOGRAPHY

Jonathan Bardon — Belfast; an Illustrated History. — 1982 & 1990.

J. C. Beckett & R. E. Glasscock — Belfast ; Origin & Growth of an Industrial City. — 1967.

J. C. Beckett et al — Belfast the Making of the City 1800-1914. — 1983.

George Benn — History of the Town of Belfast. — 1823.

George Benn — A History of the Town of Belfast: Two vols. — 1887 & 1880.

Frederick W. Boal — Shaping of a City ; Belfast in the Late Twentieth Century. — 1995.

Andrew Boyd — Holy War in Belfast. — 1969 & 1987.

C. E. B. Brett — Buildings of Belfast 1700-1914. — 1967 & 1985.

D. A. Chart — The Drennan Letters 1776-1819. — 1931.

S. J. Connolly — The Oxford Companion to Irish History. — 1998.

L. R. Crescent — In Old Belfast. — 1924.

John S. Crone — Concise Dictionary of Irish Biography. — 1937.

Estyn Evans — Pre-History and Early Christian Ireland; a Guide. — 1966.

Fred Heatley — Henry Joy MCCracken and His Times. — 1967.

Fred Heatley — The Story of St. Patrick's Belfast, 1815-1977. — 1977

Paul Larmour — Belfast; An Illustrated Architectural Guide. — 1987.

W. A. Maguire — Living Like a Lord; the Second Marquis of Donegall 1769-1844. — 1984.

W. A. Maguire — Belfast. — 1993.

J. P. Mallory & T. E. McNeill — The Archaeology of Ulster from Colonization to Plantation. — 1991.

S. Shannon Millin — Sidelights on Belfast History. — 1932.

S. Shannon Millin — Additional Sidelights on Belfast History. — 1938.

Cathal O'Byrne — As I Roved Out. — 1946.

D. J. Owen — History of Belfast. — 1921.

Marcus Patton — Central Belfast; A Historical Gazetteer. — 1993.

John Stevenson — A Frenchman's Walk Through Ireland 1796-7. — 1917.

R. M. Young — The Town Book of Belfast 1613-1816. — 1892.

R. M. Young — Historical Notices of Old Belfast and its Vicinity. — 1896.

R. M. Young — Belfast and the Province of Ulster in the 20th Century. — 1909.

plus numerous Belfast Street directories.

ACKNOWLEDGEMENT.

My wife, Stella, has had to endure with my madness for many years
and to her I would dedicate my share of this work.

Dear Reader

We hope you have found this book both enjoyable and useful. This is just one of our range of illustrated titles. Other areas currently featured include:–

Cottage

Publications

Strangford Shores
Dundalk & North Louth
Armagh

Donegal Highlands
Drogheda & the Boyne Valley
The Mournes

Also available in our "Illustrated History & Companion Range" are:-

Ballycastle and the Heart of the Glens
Larne and the Road to the Glens
Coleraine and the Causeway Coast
Bangor
Ballymoney
Lisburn
Newtownards

Ballymena
Banbridge
City of Derry
Hillsborough
Holywood
Newry

The paintings featured in each of the above titles are also available as signed artists prints.

If you require any further information please call or fax us on (01247) 883876, E-Mail us on cottage_publ@online.rednet.co.uk or write to:–

Cottage Publications
15 Ballyhay Road
Donaghadee, Co. Down
N. Ireland, BT21 0NG